125147

Brett, Vanessa.
    Phaidon guide to pewter / Vanessa
Brett. -- Englewood Cliffs, N.J. :
Prentice-Hall, c1983.
    256 p. : ill. (some col.) ; 22
cm.

    "A Spectrum book."
    Bibliography: p. 246-247.
    Includes index.
    ISBN 0-13-662049-3

    1. Pewter. I. Title.

NK8404.B74 1983   739.533

                                    83-3318
                                    AACR2 MARC

Library of Congress
21916 *62 11354   873055   © THE BAKER & TAYLOR CO.   4070

PHAIDON GUIDE TO
PEWTER

VANESSA BRETT

A SPECTRUM BOOK

Prentice-Hall, Inc., Englewood Cliffs, New Jersey 07632

Library of Congress Cataloging in Publication Data

Brett, Vanessa
   Phaidon guide to pewter

   "A Spectrum Book"
   Bibliography: p.
   Includes index.
   1. Pewter   I. Title
ISBN 0–13–662049–3
ISBN 0–13–662031–0 (pbk.)

Frontispiece A *Stegkanne* by Abraham Ganting of Berne; c. 1740,12in high, with contemporary inscription for a presentation.

Originally published by Phaidon Press Ltd, Littlegate House, St Ebbe's Street, Oxford

Planned and produced by Equinox (Oxford) Ltd
© 1982 Equinox (Oxford) Ltd

This book is available at a special discount when ordered in bulk quantities. Contact Prentice-Hall, Inc., General Publishing Division, Special Sales, Englewood Cliffs, N.J. 07632.

This edition © 19f   y Prentice-Hall, Inc., Englewood Cliffs, New Jersey 07632

A SPECTRUM BOᴜ ᴋ

10 9 8 7 6 5 4 3 2 1

ISBN 0-13-662049-3

ISBN 0-13-662031-0 {PBK.}

Printed in Hungary
Illustrations originated by Contemporary Lithoplates Ltd, London and Siviter Smith Offset Ltd, Birmingham

Prentice-Hall International, Inc., *London*
Prentice-Hall of Australia Pty. Limited, *Sydney*
Prentice-Hall Canada Inc., *Toronto*
Prentice-Hall of India Private Limited, *New Delhi*
Prentice-Hall of Japan, Inc., *Tokyo*
Prentice-Hall of Southeast Asia Pte. Ltd., *Singapore*
Whitehall Books Limited, *Wellington, New Zealand*
Editora Prentice-Hall do Brasil Ltda., *Rio de Janeiro*

CONTENTS

Pewter is a metal which is nowadays too often neglected but which, for many centuries, played an important part in people's lives. It is associated with warmth and good company – long evenings spent by a kitchen hearth, splendid dinners and everyday meals, with the good fellowship of tavern, public house, club or society, with travellers and with church ceremony. Why is it, then, that pewter is forgotten today? It is because pewter lost its place in everyday life to china and glass; because it was constantly melted down to be re-made into new articles; because it took second place to silver; because the same traditional shapes have been used time and again as expensive moulds passed from generation to generation of pewterers, too costly to be refashioned, causing some pewter design to stagnate. But it is precisely this homeliness, this continuance of tradition, that is so appealing and which makes the "feel" for pewter so important an attribute for any collector.

This book is intended as a handbook. It shows part of the enormous range of pieces that have been made, in most of the major pewter-producing countries, in the hope that collectors will look beyond their own national boundaries – a restriction which so many people have adhered to in the past.

The bulk of pewter available to the collector is from the 18th century and later, but 17th century pewter does still appear on the market. For this reason the main text concentrates on pewter made from about 1600, while items made before that date – now almost exclusively in museums – are discussed only briefly in the early part of the book. There is a small section on pewter being made today, in the hopes that it will encourage those who do not yet know about it to find out more, to buy and commission contemporary pewter and so help to maintain the traditional craft.

The interested amateur will find little pewter in general antique shops and private houses compared with the vast quantities of porcelain, silver and furniture – it tends to be sold by specialist dealers and auction houses. What he or she most probably will see in small shops are "hard metal" pieces and modern reproductions of earlier pewter. No amount of reading can teach someone to distinguish the old from the new – only experience and handling of pieces can do that.

This book makes no pretence to be a work of deep research. It is meant to be an introduction and a working guide. Those who wish to enquire further must look to the volumes listed in the bibliography and then to others not mentioned here. To the authors of those books, I extend my thanks for arousing my interest and extending my knowledge; but especial thanks go to David Walter-Ellis.

Vanessa Brett

A group of fine English pewter from The Worshipful Company of Pewterers, London. **1** A charger, dated 1676, diameter 28in, border 5in. **2** A 15th-century alms dish, centred by an enamelled boss bearing the royal coat-of-arms, 9¾in.
3 Late 16th-century flagon, from the church of the Holy Rood, Woodeaton, Oxfordshire, 12½in. **4** Tankard, c. 1700.
5 Candlestick with trumpet base, c. 1650–60, 10¾in.
6 Beaker with relief decoration incorporating the initials and motto of Henry Prince of Wales, son of James I, 1610–12, 6in.
7 Measure, 2nd half of 16th century, 5¼in. **8** Tankard, c. 1650–90. **9** Trencher salt, c. 1710. **10** Caudle cup, c. 1670. **11** Wine taster, initialled CR, early 17th-century, 2¾in. **12** Capstan salt, c. 1680.
13 Double-eared porringer with relief decoration, c. 1690–1702.

INTRODUCTION

COLLECTING PEWTER

When forming a collection the most important criterion is to buy only what you like. Do not buy purely for investment and do not buy something which is fashionable but not really to your taste. The guidance of a knowledgeable and trustworthy person, whether friend, dealer or auctioneer, can be enormously helpful. He may deter you from an unwise purchase – either because it is wrong or because it is too expensive – and an experienced guide will help to form your taste and judgement and may help you towards a successful purchase which you lack the courage to make yourself. Never be persuaded to buy something against your will – remember that the final decision on any purchase must be yours. Many people prefer to buy on their own without advice, learning by experience.

Most important of all, you must handle as many pieces as possible in order to get the *feel* of pewter – its texture, weight, method of construction, design. Instinctively you will come to know whether a piece feels right. Try to look at the marks last, so that they are a confirmation of what your eye and touch have told you regarding style, date and provenance, rather than the point from which you begin to enquire. As Francis Felten says, "seeing is more than just looking at things. Seeing is absorbing..."

Certain types of pewter will, if not properly looked after, sometimes form an oxide which at first discolours the metal, then forms a crust, which flakes. Damp and cold can affect tin, corroding the metal so that in time it disintegrates ("tin pest"). If you are uncertain how to clean a piece in poor state it is best to give it to an expert. He may well use a light application of hydrochloric acid or caustic soda, before finishing off with the finest grade of emery paper and then polishing. Recently experiments have been carried out with a method of glass bead blasting to remove oxide – using much the same principles as in sand blasting. Cleaning needs experience and a delicate touch, for it is easy to spoil a piece by being over-zealous. Some people overclean a piece, leaving the metal clean but grey and dull. Such heavy cleaning is unacceptable, for it destroys the patina which develops with age on a well-cared-for piece and ruins it in the eyes of most collectors. Pewter already in good condition can be kept that way by washing in warm soapy water and then polishing with a soft duster. Never use wire wool or similar abrasive materials.

When looking at illustrations throughout this book, you will probably notice the differences in colour of the metal. To some extent this is caused by differing alloys, particularly variations in the lead content, but very often colour is related to cleaning. Surroundings affect pewter, so that mugs or dishes kept in a smokey atmosphere, for example, develop a

A Channel Islands (Jersey) measure of ½-pint capacity which is quite badly corroded but which could be cleaned; 18th century, 5¾in.

An English measure which has had its lid and thumb-piece removed and the neck extended in order to convert it from an Old English Wine Standard pint to Imperial pint capacity. The body and handle are 18th-century, the extension dates from c. 1826, when the Imperial Standard was introduced; 6in.

brownish tinge. Curious local traditions emerge – for instance the Welsh habit of placing plates on a dresser with their faces to the wall results in their cleaning the backs of plates. An appreciation of the colour and texture of the metal which develops with age, the marvellous lustre which is the essence of good pewter, is vital.

What of pieces that are "wrong"? These can be either a fake (i.e. something made deliberately to deceive) or an altered piece. They do not include reproduction work (see p. 228), although the collector must always be on the look-out for a reproduction which is being sold as "old". Altered or restored pieces are particularly hard to detect. A thumb-piece, cover or handle may have been replaced, a spout may have been added, a foot extended, a finial added when the style does not warrant one, or decoration added later by hand. On occasion some of these can be accepted as legitimate restoration if well done (although this should be taken into account when pricing a piece). Unacceptable alterations can only be detected by knowledge of what the object *should* look like and a feeling for whether it is right or wrong. (See the chapter on Marks, in particular p. 241.)

COMPOSITION OF PEWTER

Pewter is an alloy. Although in English there are two words, one to describe the alloy (pewter) and one the basic metal (tin), in many European languages there is no distinction, "étain", "tenn" or "Zinn" being used for both. Over the centuries the composition of the alloy has changed constantly, but the chief constituent is tin, with varying quantities of lead, copper, antimony and bismuth. The most controversial of these has always been lead, for its toxic properties have long been known. In order to maintain standards and to reduce the risk of lead poisoning, strict rules were laid down regarding the quality of metal to be used. These varied from region to region and had to be revised continually because of abuse.

The composition of the metal worked in the past is only one field of research where work is always in progress and producing new evidence. Sources vary in their information, particularly regarding one of the earliest ordinances relating to the standards of alloy, that issued in London in 1348. Cotterell quotes this as: " '. . . All manner of pewter, as dishes saucers platters chargers pots square cruets square chrismatories and other things that they make square or cistils that they be made of fine pewter and the measure of Brass to the Tin as much as it will receive of his nature of the same and all other things of the said craft that be wrought as pots round that pertain to the craft to be wrought of Tin with an alloy of lead to a reasonable measure and the measure of a C.tyn is XXVI lb. of lead and that is called vessels of Tin for

Four German pieces, showing variations in the colour of the metal.
Left to right A 19th-century north German flagon, 13¼ in; an 18th-century coffee pot, 8¾ in; a flagon by Johann Phillip Boler of Regensburg, dated 1739, which has been silvered, 10¾ in; a coffee pot in rococo style c. 1750–75, which has been heavily cleaned, 10¾ in.

Left A pewterer at work in the early 19th century, surrounded by various dishes, mugs, measures, coffee pots. From *The Book of English Trades,* London, 1821.

ever.' That is to say that fine pewter was to be of pure tin with an admixture of as much brass as its own nature would permit, and second quality. . . was to be a hundred-weight of tin to twenty six pounds of lead. Two years later this was to be changed to 'To one hundred weight of 112 pounds of tin, there ought to be added no more than 16lbs of lead.' '' In *Antique Pewter of the British Isles*, Michaelis quotes the calculation of the composition as 26lb of copper plus 112lb tin for "fine" pewter or sadware, and the lower standard, "lay" metal, as 112lb tin to 26lb lead.

Recent analysis by Mrs Carlson at the Henry Francis Du Pont Winterthur Museum in Delaware, however, has proved that this must be wrong, by showing that the copper content of fine pewter from the 16th century did not exceed 2%. Over the period 1650–1850 the Winterthur findings show that most flatware contained 95% tin (to within 2%), 1–1½% copper and 1–3% lead. Antimony was introduced in small quantities in the late 17th century and the amount rose to balance the fall in copper content which in the late 18th century was down to about ½%. Flagons appeared to contain an average of 92% tin, 1% copper and 3–5% lead. These high standards were not always maintained by

11

makers in the provinces or in the composition used for baluster measures, which range from 65–75% tin and 22–30% lead.

However, no doubt it was the early initiative of the London pewterers, followed as it was by rigorous control of the trade, which earned English pewter the reputation of being of the finest quality. The terms used on the continent were usually "fine", "hard" or "English" metal for the finer grades and "common" or "ordinary" for the less good metal. "Black metal" referred to a very low grade which sometimes contained up to 30% or 40% lead. Lead was usually kept to 10–15% or less, the finest quality pewter having only 2% or 3% (the third alloy being copper).

As these alloys developed and were altered to meet the needs of clients for serviceable wares and to meet the vagaries of fashion which demanded differing techniques, a harder metal evolved. In the late 18th century the intro-duction of Britannia metal, which contained tin and anti-mony, caused much controversy which continues to this day. Is it or is it not pewter? However, if the dictionary definition of pewter as being "an alloy consisting mainly of tin" is accepted, then Britannia metal can be included as one of the many different alloys which, over the centuries, have been known as pewter.

The alloy in use today contains no lead. The composition varies slightly in each country. The proportions used in the United Kingdom, for example, are 94% tin, 4% antimony and 2% copper or bismuth. This composition was laid down by the British Standards Authority in 1969, until when the official composition of pewter included approximately 3% lead. The quantity of copper and antimony is varied depen-ding on the piece to be made and whether it is cast or spun.

HOW PEWTER IS MADE

Tin is a brittle metal which splits easily if hammered on its own. The alloys of copper and antimony make it harder and more malleable. Unlike silver, pewter softens when being worked, so annealing is unnecessary. Today most pew-terers buy pewter from a supplier in blocks or in sheets (usually rolled to about 1/16in thickness) rather than under-taking the alloying process themselves.

There are two chief methods of making articles in pewter – casting and spinning. Craftsmen take many years to train and they tend to specialize in a single field – casting, spinning, metal-working, buffing or polishing. Opinion is divided regarding the relative merits of the two methods. Many people think that cast pewter is undoubtedly the best. However, although most spun pewter is light and of poor quality, being easy to mass produce, spun pewter of good quality is also now being made – of heavy gauge and requiring a very high degree of skill. Apart from these processes, individual craftsmen, not working with the large manufacturers, hammer articles from the sheet metal or, after cutting the sheet to the required shapes, solder the various pieces together to form an object.

Modern technology has inevitably brought changes in some areas of pewter manufacturing (spinning, for example, was introduced in the late 18th century), but the basic methods for casting and turning pewter are those which have been in use for hundreds of years, as can be seen through prints, particularly those in Salmon's profusely illustrated *L'Art du potier d'étain* (Paris, 1788). The most obvious changes are the various "finishes" which manufacturers now give to their work – satin, polished, antique or coloured, the last two being produced by chemical processes.

Casting. There are several methods of casting in use today including gravity die casting (the traditional and most widely practised method of casting from gun-metal moulds); casting by centrifugal force in a rubber mould (a modern technique used for making detailed small items, chiefly models); sand casting (used principally for sculpture); and the lost-wax method (suitable only for individual items).

Manufacturers who gravity die cast pewter are frequently using moulds made over a hundred years ago. Most of the moulds are of gun metal (bronze), but steel moulds are sometimes made today. The mould is coated with a mixture of red ochre, ground pumice and white of egg; this ensures that the metal will flow easily and not stick to the mould. One coating lasts for up to 250 castings. The warm mould is held at an angle and molten pewter is ladled in, the craftsman slowly bringing the mould upright as it fills. The metal hardens in about ten seconds, so an even fast flow is vital – it is kept molten at the low temperature of 300°C (572°F). Because of this it is not usually necessary to clamp the parts of the mould together.

Each part is cast separately – the body (sometimes in two pieces, in which case the join is always on the apex of the curve), spout, base, handle, cover, hinge, finial – and then soldered together. Soldering pewter is particularly difficult because of its low melting point, which is little different to that of solder. Before adding the handle to a mug, for example, the rough casting of the body is turned on a lathe to shape and clean it. At this point any decorative incisions or mouldings are added and the piece is planed off to give it the required finish. Again, this is highly skilled work, as for much of the time (when turning the interior of pieces) the craftsman is unable to see precisely what he is doing, and relies entirely on touch.

Handles are usually made by slush casting. The molten

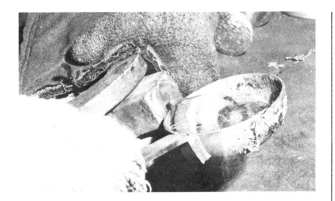

The traditional and most widely used method of casting is gravity die casting. Vessels are usually cast in several portions, the base of a tankard being the part shown here. The mould is held at an angle and as the molten metal is poured the mould is slowly tipped upright. The metal hardens in some 10 seconds.

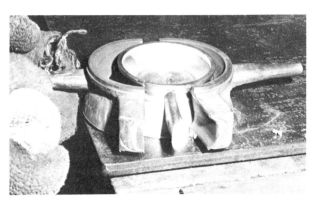

metal is ladled into a mould which is then tipped up so that metal runs out, leaving a hollow casting.

Finally the piece is polished by hand, using French chalk and a soft duster.

Centrifugal casting uses circular moulds made from synthetic heat-resistant rubber. The two halves of the mould are dusted with talc, to facilitate release from the mould and then clamped together. The upper half has a central hole from which channels run to the cavities which are to be filled with metal. The mould is rotated at high speed on a turntable and molten pewter poured in.

Spinning. Spinning is a process by which metal is placed in a lathe and forced over a wood or plastic chuck to the required shape. The body of a piece can be formed in two ways. In one, sheet metal cut to the required shape is seamed, to make a cylinder, and then briefly turned on a lathe. This method is fast and used to produce the cheapest mugs. In the other, a flat circular sheet of metal is placed in the lathe and, pressure being exerted with a spinning tool, is forced

Turning on the lathe is used to clean off the rough edges of the casting and, after the symmetrical parts have been soldered together, to give the desired finish – polished, satin, etc. – before the piece is completed by hand.

Forming a vessel by spinning. In this method of making a pewter object, a flat disc of metal is placed in the lathe and forced with spinning tools against a chuck of the required shape. The tools are shaped like large screwdrivers with the blade-tips sharpened.

into the required shape. This can be done in several stages before the final shape is achieved. Additional parts of a piece of hollow-ware are made in different ways: handles and spouts are cast but the cover and finial (of a coffee pot, for example) are spun separately.

The piece is then sand buffed to polish it, to remove any trace of a seam (if the first method is used) and to close metal pores. The piece can be finished on a lathe or given a satin or polished finish by high speed polishing using a mop impregnated with grease. A different mop is used for each type of finish.

EARLY PEWTER

Tin is mined today in Malaysia, Thailand and Indonesia, Bolivia, China and the U.S.S.R., Australia, Nigeria, South Africa, and still, to a small extent, in the British Isles. On a rough estimate, 5,000 out of 200,000 tonnes of tin mined today is used for pewter.

The days when Cornish mines produced a high proportion of the world's supply of tin are long past, but the mines there

INTRODUCTION

have been worked since Roman times. In Germany, tin was mined in the Erzgebirge in Bohemia and Saxony from the 13th century and became the main source of German tin, their busiest period being the 17th century. Tin from the east, now so important, has been mined since the early 16th century. Earlier, the Phoenicians knew of Spanish tin and the Romans also mined in Spain.

The Romans produced pewter, albeit with an enormous variety of lead contents, and a number of examples are now to be seen in museums. Thereafter, there is a large gap in our knowledge of pewter until the early Middle Ages. Only a handful of pieces of religious pewter from the 11th and 12th centuries have survived, mainly items which were buried with ecclesiastics – and some pilgrims' badges.

Paintings are a useful source to discover not only what pewter vessels looked like in the 13th, 14th and 15th centuries, but also to see how and where they were used. At this time most domestic utensils were made of wood or coarse pottery, with only the richer households using pewter or plate. Gradually the balance changed and the use of pewter became more widespread. The range of objects which have survived from the 14th and 15th centuries includes chiefly dishes, jugs or flagons and spoons, as well as ecclesiastical pewter such as cruets. Dishes were placed in the centre of the table, laden with bread and meat, from which people helped themselves, eating with their fingers or using their own knives. Drink was poured from flagons into wood or horn beakers. As table manners became more refined, ewers and basins were introduced to wash hands during the meal, and smaller plates for individual use and for sauces began to be used. Vast quantities of food and drink were consumed by those who could afford it, and heavy drinking was commonplace with much of the population, it being the most popular form of escapism from the harsh way of life endured by the poor. Pewter was the natural companion to all this. Houses were sparsely furnished in those days with benches or the occasional chair to sit on; the pewter would have been laid out on plain trestle or oak tables and dressers or stored on wall shelves.

From the 14th century we know of fine Gothic flagons from France and Switzerland, examples of which are in the Victoria and Albert Museum, the Rijksmuseum and the Landesmuseum, Zurich, and cruets of this period have been found in the English Midlands. Although the Gothic period stylistically united much of northwest Europe, from early times regional characteristics emerged in the design of flagons, tankards and pots. The slightly later group of small compact flagons known as "Hanseatic" flagons, of the 14th to 16th centuries, derives from the coastal towns of north Germany and the Low Countries which formed the Hanse-

Top The hammer-man, or maker of flatware, and *below* the pewterer or pewter pot-maker; 19th-century engravings from the woodcuts of Jost Amman's *Der Kandelgiesser*, Frankfurt-am-Main, 1568.

The compact squat form of a flagon of the "Hanseatic" type; 14th/15th century.

A gothic flagon of octagonal form with a lion sejant finial; French, 2nd half 14th century, 11in.

atic League. They have a very squat bulbous outline, are generally broad-based and sometimes bear religious medallions inside the lid or base. Early flagons were cast in vertical sections and, when made too thin, were weaker structurally than the late form of horizontal casting which was introduced in the 16th century. Flasks were made for travellers, usually of flattened circular form with a slender neck. These came to be known as pilgrims' flasks. The style was adapted for use indoors by the addition of a spreading foot. These pieces too sometimes bore cast medallions or decorative motifs on the sides. Particularly fine examples are known in France and Switzerland. Early pewter shares a wonderful simplicity of form, combining solidity with natural elegance – features which resulted in pieces of an immense charm which no other period ever achieved.

The Hanseatic flagons are some of the best known excavated pieces, dug up from river beds and shipwrecks. But pewter is constantly being retrieved from shipwrecks, river beds, old refuse tips and buildings, each find adding to our knowledge and appreciation of early pewter. Pieces so

INTRODUCTION

discovered have an additional glamour, a sense of history and a certain mystery attached to them. Some of the most notable excavated items include pewter recovered at Novaya Zemlya (see p. 144) and pewter from Port Royal in Jamaica, the thriving town which was submerged by earthquakes and tidal waves in 1692. The majority of the 200-odd pieces recovered there are English, but a French and a Dutch measure have also been retrieved from the mud. Less well preserved are the very few items recovered from *HMS Association*, flagship of Rear-Admiral Sir Cloudesley Shovell, which sank off the Scilly Isles on October 21, 1707, including one of the earliest English examples of chamberpot to have survived. Among other excavated pewter are the three candlesticks found in the moat of a 16th-century house at Arley, Lancashire, when it was being drained and cleared, and items discovered on the site of Henry VIII's famous palace of Nonesuch in Surrey, or retrieved from the wreckage of his finest warship *Mary Rose*, which sank in 1545.

As the houses of the growing middle classes became more comfortable and domestic life more congenial, pewter was in greater demand as the material most suitable for daily use. It ousted wood and pottery in people's homes. And as table manners became more polished, pewterers extended

Two pieces which convey the compactness and appeal of early pewter: *left* A Viennese tankard of the late 16th century, 4¾in; *right* a tankard from 's Hertogenbosch, dating from the 1st half of the 16th century, 5½in.

Above right Three English candlesticks which date from the 1st half of the 17th century and earlier. Items such as these are still being excavated and continually add to our knowledge of early pewter.

Right An inkstand presented to St Bartholomew's Hospital, London, dated 1619, maker's touch T.L. This is one of the earliest standishes to have survived in either pewter or silver.

the range of items they made to satisfy demand for greater elegance. By the 17th century sets of plates for individuals as opposed to serving were becoming more commonplace, and accompanied larger serving platters. However, pewter was but part of ever-changing modes of living. Just as it had ousted wood and pottery, pewter had to give way to glass, porcelain and good quality earthenware which were easier to clean and, because of the gaiety of their decoration involving the use of bright colours and pretty motifs, had greater general appeal.

For many centuries pewter had been *the* material in most common use: where we now take a glass of water, formerly we would have drunk from a pewter beaker; where now we put endless china plates into the sink or dishwasher, previously hours were spent scouring pewter plates with straw and sand; where now we have beer bought in bottles, previously our pewter mugs were filled from pewter flagons. (Even though pewter was in decline for many years, with fewer pewterers working everywhere, those which did continue in business stocked an enormous range of items even as late as 1850. In England, Townsend and Compton's catalogue included about 70 categories which, when all variations of size and shape are counted, incorporated about 350 different items.)

The pewter vessels made until well into the 19th century can be divided roughly into two categories – ecclesiastical and secular. The latter grouping can be divided into a number of sections according to use: domestic, tavern, guild and corporation. In many instances this division is arbitrary – flagons of similar style were used in all groupings and sometimes it is only an inscription which gives a clear indication of the original function of a piece. But flagons, dishes, tankards, cruets, chalices, spoons – all that multitude of objects which can so loosely be defined as either hollow-ware or flatware – are not the only use to which pewter was put. It was, and is, used to make jewellery. Organ pipes were often made of pewter, and it was used as an inlay in furniture. Tables, cabinets and doors are seen containing intricate patterns in pewter as an alternative to silver, brass or various woods. This idea was sometimes reversed, particularly in Germany where pewter flagons and measures were inlaid with copper or brass (see pp. 23 and 104).

THE PEWTER GUILDS

The guild system was well established in several countries by the 14th century. These guilds (or livery companies as they are known in London) are immensely important, not only because of the control they had over their respective trades and the lives of their members, but also because so much of the pewter which has survived from the mid–17th

Above Flagon of the Boot-makers Guild, attributed to Paulus Öham the younger, Nuremberg (25in). The shield is engraved with a shoe, emblem of the guild, and the body with names of some of its members added at various times, including 1655, 1794, 1828 and 1833.

Right A municipal or town council flagon from Amsterdam; early 17th century, 30in.

INTRODUCTION

century was made for guilds or for municipal functions in which guild members played so important a part.

As early as the 12th century workers in the same or allied trades grouped together, living close to one another and attending the same church. In Germany a guild of pewterers was founded in Nuremberg in 1285, in Augsburg in 1324 and in Hamburg in 1375. Records show that guild rules were laid down in Sweden in 1485, although the oldest ordinance of the Swedish pewterers' company, regarding the striking of a maker's touch, is dated 1545. In France, Paris led the way with a guild in 1268; other towns which supported pewterers' guilds included Strasbourg in 1363 and Dijon in 1478.

It is not until the 14th century that there are extensive and accurate records of guilds' activities. In England in 1348 the craft or fellowship of pewterers in London was sufficiently powerful to gain official recognition. Edward III granted them a royal privilege in 1363 and in 1473 Edward IV granted them a charter. This gave the Pewterers' Guild the power to control the trade, and this power extended throughout the country, even though other towns, such as York, Bristol and Edinburgh, soon established guilds of their own. In smaller centres, such as Ludlow, pewterers were one of many trades which banded together in Guilds of Hammermen. Other trades represented included goldsmiths, carpenters, coopers, blacksmiths and saddlers. This communal system existed in the Low Countries too. Although there is ample documentary evidence to show that pewterers were frequently issuing ordinances regarding quality and marking of pewter from the 14th century, the Amsterdam pewterers, for example, did not form a separate guild until 1533.

Undoubtedly the height of the guilds' powers throughout Europe came in the 15th and 16th centuries. They regulated the quality of metal and authorized the various marking systems, which had to be reaffirmed or altered frequently. They checked on prices, wages and hours of work, and they organized apprenticeship. In some areas the interest of the guild extended into the private lives of members too: whom they married, which church they attended and which taverns they frequented.

The apprenticeship system varied from country to country and from town to town. To take London as an example, the length of apprenticeship was at least seven years. Once this period of training was completed, the apprentice was presented by his master to the court of the Pewterers' Company. He had to present a test piece to show his work and he had to prove that he had sufficient funds to set up a business of his own. Only then was he permitted to strike his touch and be admitted to the Company in his own right. Gradually as the years passed he could work his way up the hierarchy of the Company – from freeman to liveryman,

Two examples of the *cimarre* flagon, most of which were made in France in the 17th and 18th centuries; 9½ and 11in.

A 19th-century flask, made in earlier style, by Carl Gotthold Breitfeld of Annaberg in Saxony; 8½in.

steward, warden and master.

The London Company sent searchers to scour the provinces, checking the quality of items sold and destroying them if they failed to come up to standard. Concern about the protection of workers from imported wares was a problem with which every town in every country had to contend. Everyone was very happy to export wares but worried about competition from workers who did not belong to the local guilds. The London pewterers were no different from any other livery company, and feelings against foreign workers ran high. The opinion expressed by one writer in 1577 regarding the importation of foreign textiles, for example, that "we ought to favour the strangers from whom we learnt so great benefits, because we are not so good devisers as followers of others" was very much a minority view.

It is perhaps easier to appreciate the camaraderie of guild life on the continent than in England, for a reasonable quantity of guild pewter still exists from Germany, the Low Countries, France and Switzerland, whereas very little has

Guild pewter: *left* a German guild tankard in silvered pewter by Paul Weise of Zittau, Saxony; second half 16th century, 20½in. The handle and body are cast in relief with mythical and allegorical figures from models by Peter Flotner; the body has three shields applied at the front. *Right* The guild cup of the pewterers' guild of Lübeck, of pewter inlaid with brass, dated 1717; 32⅓in.

INTRODUCTION

survived in England. Some of the finest pewter of the 15th, 16th and 17th centuries has connections with guilds or town councils. Many of these cups and flagons are inscribed with the name of the guild, its members and its emblem. Dinners were frequently held at which members had their own tankards filled from enormous flagons. Sometimes these flagons were so large that it was impossible to lift them when filled, so a tap was inserted near the base. Toasts were drunk and on arrival a visitor was greeted with the welcome cup (*Willkomm*) from which everybody drank. Some of the cups were made in the shape of emblems of the guilds – a shoe for bootmakers, a bull for butchers or a twisted loaf for bakers. These emblems were also shown in guild shields, which were hung outside taverns (or inside, over a specific table), to guide a man to his fellow workers. A simple example is illustrated on p. 26; others are far more elaborate. The benefits of travel and experience which could be gained from contact with other peoples was fully appreciated on the continent. Most pewterers travelled as part of their apprenticeship before settling down and joining a guild.

The flagons which were displayed and used at guild and municipal functions vary enormously stylistically. In France the *cimarre* or *cimaise* was both an attractive and a popular vessel. In the Low Countries and Germany many flagons had a bulbous body, a slender cylindrical neck, and rested on a high trumpet base. Those from Regensburg are particularly distinctive. Further east, in Silesia, Moravia, Bohemia and Hungary, cylindrical flagons, often faceted, rest on cast feet of human or animal form. The body was often covered with elaborately engraved, cast or stamped decoration. Many of these pieces are very large – 20–30in high. The flattened flask or *bouteille* is found in the Rhineland of both France and Germany, and in Switzerland. Switzerland's most characteristic vessel was the spouted council flagon, ancestor of the *Stegkanne*, with a central swing handle as well as a loop handle opposite the spout. These flagons often have cast shields or medallions on the body, bearing the arms of the town or owner.

By the early 18th century the power of the guilds was failing. Workers began to resent interference in their work by the courts of the guilds and paid less attention to the rules. The courts could no longer afford expensive searches. The London Pewterers' Company became cautious about sending men to places where there were thriving local trades, whose members naturally resented interference from the capital. By the mid-18th century the Company had virtually ceased to control the trade. The enormous and no doubt riotous dinners which were so important a part of early guild and municipal life were held less frequently. Perhaps they became more formal as manners became more refined and

A town council flagon from Regensburg, Bavaria; 1660.

standards of living rose. They also became more expensive. The traditional feast which, in some guilds, a member had to give when admitted master had long been abolished because it proved a crippling expense for someone just launched on a career. Instead, he often had to present a piece of pewter to the guild. The French Revolution sounded the death knell for guilds in France – the Low Countries and Germany followed suit and also abolished them. The Worshipful Company of Pewterers, along with 82 other livery companies, still thrives in the City of London, taking part in matters connected with their trade. Since the last war, the Company has built up a fine study collection of British pewter.

A municipal flagon from Zug, Switzerland, dated 1592–1657. The carrying-handle is iron; 16¼in.

Next page A group of mainly Dutch and German pewter, mostly of the 18th and 19th centuries. *Top left* is a Dutch beaker with "wriggled" engraving; the *bottom row* includes the sign of a shoemaker's guild dated 1804, a Dutch round-bowled spoon, a double-compartment spice box and a German figure candlestick.

But in the place of the guilds new organizations have arisen. Although the guild system was never introduced to America, the American Pewter Guild, founded in 1958, now actively promotes the trade. In the United Kingdom the Association of British Pewter Craftsmen has 30 manufacturing members – either companies or individuals. In Germany there is the Gutegemeinschaft Zinngerat, and in Belgium the Belgian Pewter Association (Chambre Syndicale des Maîtres Étainiers de Belgique) was formed in 1974.

PERIOD STYLES

Most pewter can be categorized into (a) those pieces which have the feel and tradition of local pewter, whose shapes are unique to pewter with no thought for other areas of the arts, namely measures, and (b) those pieces which reflect styles and decorative features of the period, principally those of goldsmiths.

Many people are struck unfavourably by the plainness and simplicity of pewter, and think it dull. The pewterer did indeed rely on proportion and balance to convey quality and sound workmanship, but if the rarer and more richly ornamented pewter, which was bought only by the wealthy middle classes, was more often met with, it could not really be considered dull.

Throughout the following chapters reference is frequently made to contemporary styles and fashions in silver, or to the work of goldsmiths. What exactly is meant by this? To quote the historian William Harrison (1534–93), "our pewterers in times past employed the use of pewter only upon dishes and pots, now they are grown into such exquisite cunning they can in manner imitate any form or fashion of cup, dish, salt, bowl or goblet that is made by goldsmiths craft, though they be ever so curious, exquisite or artificially forged."

Although every region develops its own local characteristics in terms of stylistic detail, western culture has always been subject at any one time to one predominant influence which has dominated the work of artists. These influences spread via artists themselves as they travelled, by the exchange of gifts between rulers which were then seen and copied by local craftsmen, and by the use of engraved designs, which were circulated in books and sheets of ornament, so that woodcarvers, cabinet makers, pewterers and goldsmiths all borrowed ideas from designers such as Virgil Solis, Hopfer, van Vianen, Étienne Delaune, Jean Bérain. Whereas during the Renaissance inspiration came from Italy, in the 17th and 18th centuries Germany, the Low Countries and France were most influential.

The *gothic* style of the 12th to 15th centuries is characterized in the soaring arches and delicate tracery of its architecture which, when transferred to furniture and metal

work, gives a vertical emphasis. In pewter this is most clearly seen in simple but majestic flagons, and in chalices, where hexagonal or octagonal bases taper and rise towards the bowl.

The 15th century saw the development of the Renaissance, which at first had little effect on pewter. However, by the mid-16th century a refinement emerged known as *mannerism*. As its name suggests, mannerism is characterized by stylishness; figures, both human and animal, are linked by strapwork, entwined foliage and grotesques. These were the forms chosen by François Briot and his followers to produce the elaborate cast work known as *Edelzinn* (pp. 68–71, 93–5).

The sinuous forms of mannerism developed in the 17th century into the opulent *baroque*. Now the entwined foliage becomes fuller and more natural; putti play with dolphins, lions and shells amid a riot of leafage. Pewter plates, particularly, feature this style in borders, both engraved and in relief, including tulips and other flowerheads.

The exuberance of baroque was tamed in France during the reign of Louis XIV. Now the *classical* forms mingle with the richness of ornament which Louis' court inspired and it dominated European taste – assiduously promoted by emigré Huguenot craftsmen. In pewter, plates, salvers and salts, for example, were given gadrooned, corded and beaded borders and hollow-ware was applied with strap

Left A tankard by Isaac Faust of Strasbourg (1606–69); 7in. The design of this tankard is similar to those made by Caspar Enderlein (compare illustration p. 95).

Above A fine English tankard, engraved in "wrigglework" with portrait busts of Mary II and her husband William III who came to the throne in 1689; 6½in.

Right A pair of candlesticks by Benjamin Cooper of London, c. 1680, 11in, the bases 8½in wide.

Below right An 18th-century German plate with deeply moulded border and attractive engraving.

Below An early 18th-century caster, with an elaborately pierced cover; probably French.

work and moulded girdles. But this was also the time (1680–1710) when *wrigglework* engraving was most popular on pewter, particularly in England and the Low Countries, where the naive execution of portraits, wildlife and foliage shows such charm. In Germany, Switzerland and Scandinavia, this wriggled ornament was executed throughout the 18th century with greater sophistication.

Asymmetry and naturalism, which were the basis of *rococo*, were ideally suited to the decorative arts. Each piece, whether candlestick, ewer or bowl, was moulded into swirling curves. (Some rococo pieces have simpler vertical fluting or "straight-fold" decoration.) Whilst the nature of

pewter vessels did not permit the pewterers to take rococo to the extremes seen in porcelain, silver and interior design, they nevertheless accepted the new fashion wholeheartedly in some countries. The style was never used by English pewterers (although obviously they were aware of its possibilities as is misleadingly shown in some trade cards). The Dutch used it sparingly, as did the French, who used it as surface decoration rather than as an integral part of the design. Only the Germans experimented with the style to any large degree. Rococo simply did not suit everyone's taste and during the period of its greatest popularity (1725–60) we find that the majority of English and Dutch pieces are of surprising simplicity, such as the candlestick illustrated.

After the wildness of rococo, reaction set in in the form of *neo-classicism*. Again very popular in metalwork, its elegance particularly appealed to the northern tastes of pewterers in Scandinavia and the Low Countries, and to a lesser degree in England. The restrained outlines of neo-classicism are enlivened by garlands of husk motifs and

Dutch candlestick, c. 1730, with faceted baluster stem, matching sconce and base. The nozzle on this example is fixed, but many are detachable.

Left A group of rococo pewter, mostly German; mid-18th century.

Rococo. *Right* A pair of candlesticks decorated with swirling flutes, probably Dutch, mid-18th century.

Below A ewer, with straight-fold decoration. Probably German, mid-18th century; 8¼in.

Right Neo-classical: a covered bowl, with portrait medallions pendant from laurel festoons, 8¼in, and a pair of candlesticks with Corinthian column stems, the base with bands of anthemions and beading below similar portrait busts; 11½in. All late 18th-century Dutch. (The candlestick nozzles should be of matching square form.)

INTRODUCTION

classical busts, which reflect the architectural designs of the period.

The classical inspiration which was so strong in late 18th-century design was given a new dimension by the influence of Egypt. Sphinxes, lyres, anthemions and palms bordered and girdled domestic articles such as tea urns, coffee pots, salt cellars and bowls. This is the *Empire* style, particularly popular in France and Germany, during Napoleon's years of power. Pewterers enjoyed a short-lived revival in business while this fashion lasted. Thereafter the popularity of pewter waned and so too did the desire of the few remaining pewterers to keep abreast of fashion. During the 19th century the Biedermeier era in Austria c. 1830–40, the period of the Second Empire in France (1852–71), and the stylistic revivals of naturalism and gothicism, had very little effect on domestic items made in pewter. Only at the end of the century, with the influence of *Art Nouveau*, was pewter once again used to portray contemporary fashion.

TRADITIONAL PEWTER

These then, are the basic features of form and ornament which pewterers used to produce fashionable pieces which would in some measure compete with other materials. But what of those other forms, usually local and confined to pewter, which are rather vaguely described as "traditional" pewter?

As has already been said, it is important to develop a "feel" for pewter, so that reference to any marks should merely be to obtain detailed information. To understand regional characteristics you must develop a feel for design and an understanding of the various elements which combine in any one piece. In flagons, for example, this includes body shape, foot, cover, handle, thumbpiece and spout. It is, of course, impossible to be dogmatic when describing stylistic features: that is why some geographical and historical knowledge is so important. Some pewterers travelled quite extensively and borrowed ideas from craftsmen in other areas, particularly if they had settled away from their native country. Trying to attribute an unmarked piece to a specific maker is often complicated by the fact that pewterers lent each other moulds because they were so expensive to make. In *A History of American Pewter*, to take just one such case, Montgomery tells how Thomas D. Boardman rented moulds from Edward Danforth.

Flagons, tankards and measures. A few of the basic designs of thumbpiece and handle are shown to illustrate the importance of this knowledge. For example, the ball thumbpiece is characteristic of Germany and Austria–Hungary; the twin-acorn is from France, Switzerland and the

Above A German coffee pot c. 1850, a late Empire piece; 9¾in.

Right Empire: a Dutch or German tea urn, on a fixed wooden base. The lyre (see the tap handle) was a frequently used form of ornament at this time; 1st quarter 19th century.

INTRODUCTION

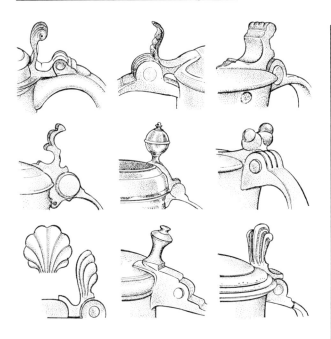

Left Thumbpieces. *Top row, left* scroll (England, North America); *centre* short erect (this one 1700, from Leiden); *right* short erect, ridged (this c. 1750, Paris). *Centre row, left* high erect (German-speaking areas); *centre* ball (German-speaking areas); *right* twin acorn (France, Switzerland, Channel Islands). *Bottom row, left* shell (chiefly Low Countries); *centre* Scandinavian ball; *right* plumed (Germany, Austria, Switzerland; simpler forms in Scandinavia).

Right Handle terminals. *Top row, left to right* ball and fishtail, 18th century; double-scroll or "broken", late 18th and 19th centuries; "attention", 19th century. All English or American. *Bottom row* the three basic methods of joining the lower handle to the body, used with minor variations almost universally on tankards and flagons; the decorated terminal (*right*) is from the Tyrol, 17th/18th century.

Below right The relief-decorated handle with ridged terminal, and double-C erect thumb-piece, also ridged, of a tankard from Joachimsthal, Germany; c. 1600.

Left Lid of a Silesian tankard, showing initials engraved in a style commonly employed in Germany and Austria.

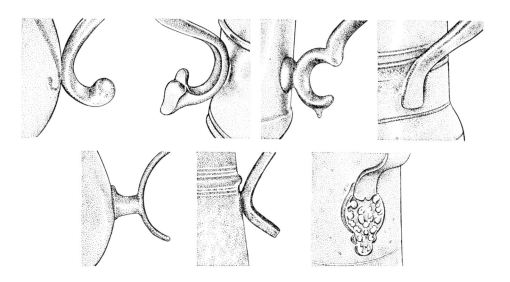

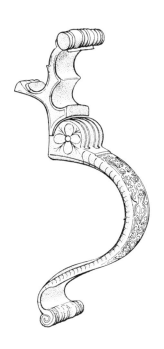

Channel Islands; the erect is found in various forms in France, the Low Countries and Germany but is not found in the British Isles except on some 17th-century flagons and on Scots tappit-hens; some Scottish measures have an embryo-shell thumbpiece, but the fully developed shell is found principally in the Low Countries. The various plumed thumbpieces are found mainly in Germany, Austria and Switzerland, with the simpler splayed forms being made in Scandinavia. In England there was tremendous variety of thumbpieces on 17th-century tankards and flagons (including a form of plume in the 1690's); measures progressed from hammerhead or ball (not to be confused with the continental ball on flagons), to bud, then double-volute.

Handles, particularly the terminals, are also of great assistance in determining the provenance and date of a piece. The basic shapes of a handle are scroll (with varieties of double-scroll or "broken") and angular (strap). The latter are found primarily on cylindrical measures or flagons from north Germany, Scandinavia, the Low Countries and France. Scroll handles either terminate in an outward curve with various terminals, or are fixed flush to the body (on English pub mugs, for example, this is known as "attention"; some Austrian measures make a feature of this junction of handle and body by applying a mask). Handles with a projecting terminal on Austrian, German, Swiss and French pieces frequently have a ridged terminal, similar to the decoration on some erect thumbpieces. Other terminals reflect contemporary silver designs, for example spade, fishtail, shield, heart, ball.

Left The variety in thumbpieces of measures and tankards was particularly marked
in England in the 17th and
18th centuries. *Top left* bud
(late 17th to 18th century) and
right double-volute (18th
century, both on wine
measures); *centre left* open
chairback (18th century) and
right bifurcated (17th
century); *bottom left* leaf
spray (17th century). The
plumed thumbpiece (*bottom
right*) was most popular in
Germany and Austria from
the 17th to 19th centuries.

These are often the principal decorative features on a
pewter flagon or tankard. Other methods of enlivening the
plain outline of a piece were the use of moulded or incised
girdles. Chasing (hammered relief decoration) was never
used extensively (one exception being work of poor quality
in France) but engraving is frequently found. "Wrigglework"
engraving, which was a universally popular technique,
achieved the desired effect by the engraver pushing a chisel-
pointed tool over the surface of the metal in a rocking
motion. The inscribing of names and armorials was usually
carried out by line engraving. Heraldic engraving was
normally excecuted by specialist engravers and not by the
pewterer, but Michaelis tells of a pewterer who, in 1588,
was fined "for that he set a stranger to work to grave upon
his pewter when he might have it wrought by a brother of
the Company".

Plates, dishes and chargers. Engraving was used to decorate flatware as well as hollow-ware. However, the principal
feature by which dishes are dated is the border. Having said
this, a feature of many early plates, which was not usually
seen in England after about 1670 and on the continent (for
example in Switzerland and Germany) after about 1720, is
the raised boss in the centre. Not only is the shape of the
border important, but also its width in relation to the overall

Right An early German plate
with narrow rim and raised
boss in the centre, 11in. The
maker's touch is dated 1633;
below it are initials added in
the 18th century.

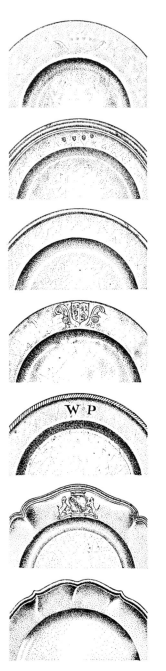

Left Plate borders, *top to bottom.* Broad-rimmed (17th century) multiple-reeded rim (late 17th/early 18th century); single-reeded rim (18th century); plain-rimmed (18th/early 19th century); corded, wavy-edged, rococo (all mid-18th century).

Above An English charger engraved with the arms of the Earls of Mount Edgecombe; c. 1640, 22¾ in.

Right Varieties of finial found on 16th- and 17th- century spoons of the type shown in full (which has an acorn finial). *Top row, left to right* wrythen; horned headdress, puritan, horseshoe. *Second row* seal top; diamond. *Bottom* maidenhead.

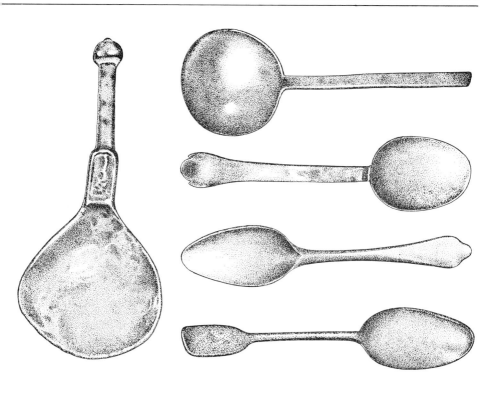

Above Fig-shaped bowl and ball terminal, Dutch/German, early 17th century

Above right, from top Frisian round-bowled, 17th century; English "trefid", c. 1660–1700; English "dog nose", c. 1690–1720; fiddle pattern, late 18th and 19th centuries.

diameter of the dish. What is impossible to convey in writing and illustration is the sheer size and weight of many of these pieces and how important proportions are in assessing their visual impact.

As a general rule the definition of flatware is as follows: plates 8–10in diameter, dishes 10–18in, chargers over 18in; saucers are anything smaller than about 6½in. The largest chargers seen today are approximately 24–26in, although chargers of 34½in are recorded.

Spoons. Collecting spoons tends to be a specialist field of collecting but this should not deter the newcomer. Building up a group of spoons to include a representative selection of finials can be a very rewarding and relatively inexpensive passtime. Many collectors of pewter also buy latten (brass) spoons. When dating a spoon it is important to look at the finial and also the shape of the bowl. Spoons are usually struck with the maker's touch inside the bowl just below the handle.

Left Spoons of the 16th and 17th centuries displayed in an English spoon rack. In the foreground is a bronze mould (c. 1690–1700) with a dog-nose spoon cast from it.

Right Judaica: a German Passover plate; mid 18th-century, 10in.

Below right A chalice made in Nuremberg in the 18th century; 7in.

INTRODUCTION

Left A group of ecclesiastical pewter, mostly 18th-century, including a holy water bucket, a holy water stoup (*bénitier*), two chrismatories, altar cruets and a crown, most probably from a statue of the Virgin or a Saint.

Below A hanukah lamp of the mid-18th century; 12½in wide.

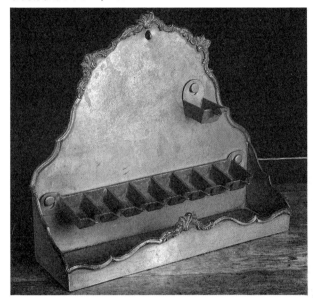

CHURCH PEWTER

Pewter made for religious use includes Christian and Jewish items. Jewish pewter comes mainly from Austria–Hungary, Germany and the Low Countries. Ceremonial items include seder dishes, suitably engraved, and hanukah lamps.

In both the Catholic and Protestant churches the majority of sacred vessels were made of precious metals. However, many of the poorer parishes were unable to afford silver and were allowed to use pewter. Obviously ecclesiastical pewter reflects contemporary style and national character-istics. In the Catholic church items most frequently found are sanctuary lamps, altar candlesticks, chalices, cruets (*burettes*), chrismatories and holy water stoups (*bénitiers*). After the Reformation, many Catholic chalices were melted in order to replace them with pieces of new design. Protes-tant communion cups usually have a deeper and more angular bowl. Communion flagons or lavers conform to local styles, as do alms dishes. They are often engraved with the sacred monogram and the name of the church. In Scotland and America, in particular, many communion sets have remained intact, probably because they were among the last to be manufactured.

43

BRITISH ISLES

Measures are virtually the only pewter made in the British Isles which do not wholly derive from the styles of silver: their baluster shape probably comes from the pottery jugs of the Middle Ages. English pewterers constantly copied the work of silversmiths. Perhaps because they knew that their pewter was of a high standard, English pewterers did not clutter their utilitarian work with frills to attract the customer, and decoration was kept to an absolute minimum. The English pewterer relied on quality and simplicity of design.

However, from the Middle Ages until the early 18th century there were often times when for a period of, say, 20 to 30 years, decorated pewter was made extensively, as can be seen in the Weoly cruet of the 13th or 14th century, in pewter of the late Elizabethan and James I era (late 16th and early 17th centuries), and, after a gap of several decades, the popular "wrigglework" pewter of the second half of the 17th century. When the fashions for wrigglework and relief-cast ornament died about 1725 not long after Anne, the last Stuart monarch, virtually the only decoration on British pewter, apart from a little moulding, was the engraving of the identity of the owner – whether it be a fairly lengthy inscription as found on Scottish communion pewter, the name of a tavern or public house, or the heraldic bearings of an aristocratic household. The nearest that English 18th-century pewterers came to following continental fashions was in the making of wavy-edged plates. They never accepted the rococo style and were not too keen on neo-classicism, although the occasional piece can be found.

Some early English pewter shows close similarities to pewter from the Low Countries, for example candlesticks and dishes; and some Scottish pewter reflects the fact that for many years Scotland had closer links with the Low Countries and France than with England. Because of the insularity of Britain, her pewter does not present the same problems for identification as pieces which come from regions spanning national boundaries on the continent, such as the Rhineland or Friesland, although within the British Isles there are regional variations, notably the pewter of Scotland, Ireland and the Channel Islands.

The range of items found today in English pewter lacks many of the objects made elsewhere, for example food containers or flasks, coffee pots (which have survived only in Britannia metal, the early examples made when pewterers elsewhere in Europe were still using traditional methods), and any quantity of guild pewter.

From Roman times, the mines of Cornwall produced ample supplies of tin for the whole country. Tin was transported by water and road, but the main centres for pewterers were either ports or on easily navigable rivers. The number of pewterers in a town reflects its changing importance through the centuries: thus, by the 18th century Norwich, Chester and Ludlow were no longer the major centres they had been in the Middle Ages; Bewdley lost favour to Birmingham and Sheffield; later Bristol suffered from the slackening of trade to America. The Civil War between Charles I and the parliamentary forces, and Cromwell's protectorate of 1649 – 60, had a less catastrophic effect on pewter than on the fine arts. Charles I's superb picture collection was broken up and vast quantities of silver were melted to pay for the war; but pewter's simplicity and worthiness were probably more in tune with Puritanism, and stylistically it did not change as radically as silver.

However, much pewter was probably lost in the war and one wonders, also, how much was lost or irreparably damaged in the Great Fire of London of 1666 – for early 17th century pewter is rare. This has led to the late 17th century being described as the period when Britain's finest pewter was made but, judging from the few earlier pieces which are left to us, there is no reason to suppose that pewter every bit as fine was not made in earlier times. We simply do not have enough to generalize about it.

The chief centres of pewter manufacture in England and Wales, Scotland, Ireland and the Channel Islands. Many of these towns, such as York, Glasgow, Edinburgh and Bristol, are known for their own style of pewter vessels.

Two plates engraved with "wriggle work"; c. 1700, 8½ and 8¾in. While both have the same design of three tulips the plate on the left is of finer quality, not only in execution but also in composition.

Left A fine Charles II commemorative charger; c. 1662, 21½in. It is engraved in the centre witht the Royal Arms and the border incorporates tulips, acorns and tudor roses.

The restoration of Charles II in 1660 produced a fine series of commemorative pieces — decorated in a style which continued through the later Stuart reigns. In the 18th century a substantial proportion of several pewterers' output was exported to America, the English pewterers being assisted by favourable laws. But by the time of American independence and the French Revolution the trade was in decline, and the great wave of political and social change which had so great an effect on their continental colleagues did not affect British pewterers to anything like the same extent. The industrial revolution was of far more importance here (see the chapter on the Nineteenth Century).

RELIEF WORK AND COMMEMORATIVE PIECES
In the late 16th and early 17th centuries England did not produce the quantity of fine relief work that is seen in France and Germany. Only a handful of such early 17th-century pieces survives, notably the well-known candlestick by William Grainger in the Victoria and Albert Museum, a few beakers and wine cups (one of which recently came to light in 1980 and bears the charming inscription "Though wine bee good too much of that wil make one lean though he be fatt"), and one or two patens. Towards the end of the 17th century there is also a group of commemorative porringers or écuelles (they have two handles) bearing portraits of William and Mary, and some portraying John Churchill, Duke of Marlborough.

Commemorative display pewter accounts for some of the finest late 17th-century pewter to have survived. Between 12 and 15 chargers are known to have been made in 1661 and 1662 which are profusely engraved with the royal arms, emblems of England and Scotland and an inscription "Vivat Rex Carolus Secundus Beati Pacifici" (or words to similar effect). These most probably commemorate Charles II's betrothment and marriage to Catherine of Braganza. For the rest of the century, a popular form of decoration, mainly on plates and tankards, was a portrait of the monarch in wrigglework engraving: Charles II, then William III and Mary II (reigned jointly 1689–1695, then William alone (1695–1702).

Although relief-cast spoons are occasionally found with portraits of George III (1760–1820), the fashion for commemorative pewter seems to have faded at the time of the Hanoverian accession in 1714.

CHARGERS, DISHES AND PLATES
An overall term used for this kind of flatware (not for cutlery) is "sadware". Sadware was often made and sold in sets, known as a "garnish", which might contain several dozen plates, soup plates, and meat dishes in various sizes,

Above Plain-rimmed plate bearing the ownership stamp of the Borough of Newbury, Berkshire; by Helier Perchard; 18th century, 9¾in. *Below* Plate with multiple-reeded rim, clearly showing "hallmarks"; by Thomas France or Francis; c. 1680, 9½in.

Left Plate with corded border, mid-18th century, by Tutin of Birmingham, 9¾in. *Right* Plain-rimmed plate by Richard Fletcher of London; c. 1690–1700, 9¼in. The crossed plumage surrounding the armorials is a typical form of decoration used with heraldry in the last 30 years of the 17th century.

sometimes together with soup tureens and sauce boats.

Very little flatware has come down to us that was made before the Civil War. The raised boss is a feature of early 17th-century plates which had virtually disappeared by about 1660. In the mid-17th century most plates and dishes had very broad rims with plain borders, although these often bore owner's initials or "hallmarks". By about 1675 the border began to be decorated with cast or incised reeding, the proportion of the border to overall diameter of the piece being slightly less than previously. This "triple-reeding" or "multiple-reeding" also appears on the rarer narrow-rimmed plates of 1675–1700. Multiple-reeded dishes were in fashion throughout the last quarter of the 17th century, before they lost favour around 1700 to the simpler single

Left Wavy-edged plate with foliate moulded rim, engraved with a crest, by Samuel Duncombe; mid-18th century. *Right* Octagonal plate, c. 1780.

reeded rim, which appeared on plates and dishes until the mid-18th century. From about 1730, however, plain-rimmed plates began to be made, which continued well into the 19th century – long after all other styles had been discontinued. The French influence resulted in a crop of attractive designs c. 1730–70, including wavy-edged, gadrooned and octagonal. These types, presumably because they were considerably more expensive, were never made in such quantities as the simpler plain-rimmed or single-reeded designs, although garnishes of wavy-edged plates and dishes are still to be found. One other style, of c. 1690–1710, has pieces with gadroon borders and includes salvers-on-foot.

Plates and dishes were frequently engraved on the rim with the crest or coat-of-arms of the owner. This always adds interest to the piece, not only because the engraving is often very attractive and enhances the piece visually, but also because it is frequently possible to trace the original owner. Sometimes you find that the plate was once part of a large garnish, other pieces of which are scattered in many collections, or that it has a particularly interesting provenance. One good example of this is a very fine group of

17th-century dishes which once belonged to the Mount Edgecumbe family of Cothele, Cornwall, in which some dishes have engraved armorials, some stamped ownership initials.

A group of early 18th-century porringers; 6½ – 7½in across the "ears".

PORRINGERS

The English porringer has a slightly convex-sided circular body and a single pierced handle, or ear. The majority of those that have survived were made between 1690 and 1730. The plain bowl design remained fairly static, except for rare relief-decorated examples (one is shown on p. 6) and the handle was always of a roughly triangular shape. However, the handle is pierced in a variety of patterns, some very simple, others more elaborate, with foliage, or incorporating dolphins and crowns in higher relief. Many of these designs were copied by American pewterers, who continued to make porringers long after they had ceased to be made in England. Marks were usually struck on the underside of the body or handle.

SPOONS

Spoon-making was a specialist skill and a different craft from that of the pewterer who made hollow-ware and sadware. Although spoons were probably the most easily destructible article used in a home – something which frequently had to be replaced because of wear and tear – a comparatively large quantity of early spoons has survived, many spoons having been excavated. Many spoonmakers worked in latten as well as in pewter, as the brass alloy is more hard-wearing than pewter.

From the 14th to the mid-17th centuries spoons were made with a variety of finials, some of the less commonly found examples being horse's hoof, maidenhead, horned head-dress, wrythen, ball, hexagon, diamond, lion sejant. More frequently seen types date from the late 16th and early 17th centuries, such as seal-top spoons, which were followed in the 17th century by the plainer slip-top and Puritan spoons. At the end of the 17th century the bowl of the spoon developed from the previous fig shape into the oval bowl which remains in present-day patterns. The terminal was flattened and shaped into the "trefid" design. This design, popular between c. 1680 and 1710, was either plain or cast in relief (notably, in the royal portrait spoons). Later styles continued to copy those of silver spoons, the trefid developing into the dog-nose, then Hanoverian and fiddle patterns. Most specialist spoon collectors find these later spoons less interesting than those of the 17th century and earlier.

The spoonmaker struck his mark in the bowl near the junction with the handle. A spoon that bears marks on the back of the bowl is likely to be a modern copy.

CANDLESTICKS

Candlesticks from the first half of the 17th century and earlier (like those illustrated on p. 19) are very rare. They resemble contemporary Low Countries pieces and, as they are usually unmarked, it is sometimes difficult to be certain of their origin. By the mid-17th century a typically English form known as the trumpet-base had evolved. Similar examples are to be found in brass and pottery. A typical later 17th-century feature of candlesticks is a wide drip-pan projecting from the mid-section of the stem just above the base. One attractive style is the octagonal-based stick with matching drip-pan and cylindrical stem. These are contemporary (1685–1700) with the pair of column candlesticks illustrated on p. 29. By this time the combined influences of emigré Huguenot craftsmen and the installation of a Dutchman on the English throne began to be felt and pewter developed stylistically along the lines of contemporary silver and pottery. At the end of the century candlesticks had become more delicate with faceted square bases rising to ball-knopped stems, or with bases of circular outline.

English pewter candlesticks made during the period 1700–80 are probably as rare as 17th-century examples, presumably the great majority of the candlestick market having been supplied by the brass founders; the examples

A late 17th-century candlestick, with octagonal base, drip-pan and sconce; c. 1675, 7½in.

known follow the same shapes as silver and brass. Towards the end of the 18th century a style of baluster candlestick evolved which continued to be made for most of the 19th century, when they were usually made in "hard metal". These candlesticks (a later example is illustrated on p. 196) had push-rod ejectors to remove the stub of the candle.

OTHER DOMESTIC WARES

For the most part items such as salts, casters, tureens, tea caddies, two-handled cups (or "loving cups"), and inkstands followed the contemporary silver styles. Late 17th-century salts are usually capstan-shaped, a style which developed around 1710–30 into the more compact "trencher" type – all these with a shallow depression to take the salt. By about 1735 the bowl had increased in size and rested on a pedestal foot. This style, known as a cup salt, continued until about 1780. Few English casters are known prior to about 1750, but from then until the mid-19th century a wide variety of baluster, vase-shaped and bun-topped casters are available to the collector (see p. 198).

Other interesting earlier pieces are occasionally discovered, such as a 17th-century wine taster or a saucer. However, most of the household wares to be seen today, which include bedpans, tobacco jars, meat dishes, strainers, and medical equipment, date from the 19th century and are discussed and illustrated in a later chapter.

Right A fine flagon with bun cover, marked on the handle, c. 1610–20; 15in.

Above An inkstand, probably late 18th-century; 4in. The upper drawer is for wafers, the lower drawer pierced for pounce. Inkwells such as these were often used in banks.

Left A two-handled or "loving" cup; 18th-century, 6in across cup.

Left A Scottish porringer or "quaich".

Below left Four "trencher" salts; c. 1700–1720, average height 1½in.

FLAGONS

With one or two rare exceptions, such as the York "acorn", English flagons from c. 1600 onwards are of cylindrical form, with variations in the lid, finial, thumbpiece, handle and foot, all of which show a natural progression in styles. It is, of course, impossible to be precise, but the dates given here are a rough guideline based chiefly on the researches of scholars such as Cotterell and Michaelis.

Although a large proportion of 17th-century flagons which have survived are undoubtedly of church origin (an ordinance of 1234 permitted the use of pewter for church vessels), the same styles must also have been made for pieces intended for secular use. From c. 1610 for some ten years, the flagon has a slender elegant body with bun cover, knop and solid erect thumbpiece, the handle projecting from below the

Above Two flagons from York, the York version of the tapering cylindrical flagon with moulded bands at the base and a domed lid (1690–1700) and the "acorn" type made in York and Wigan; 1st half 18th century, 10–12in.

Right English flagons, the muffin cover with and without finial; c. 1630, 11½ and 13¼in.

hinge. This develops into the "muffin" cover 1620–80, with or without finial and with pierced thumbpiece, often heart-pierced. Then, during 1625–40, a finial is generally present, and the handle develops a pronounced scroll at the top. From 1650 developed the popular "beefeater" flagon, bulkier in shape, the lid bearing a resemblance to the caps worn by Yeomen Warders at the Tower of London. Beefeater flagons have a variety of thumbpieces: bifurcated, twin-cusp, or heart-and-leaf spray.

At the end of the 17th century a flagon emerged which was, in effect, an extended tankard. It took a more steeply tapering form, with a simple scroll handle, a flat-topped lid often with fretted denticulations at the front, and a bifurcated thumbpiece. Variations of this type of tapering flagon continued to be made into the 18th century, usually with a moulded girdle, sometimes spouted, the thumbpiece often a simple volute or (in a late example) of chairback type.

The straight-sided York flagon of c. 1700 has multiple moulded bands near the base, and usually a domed cover with the typical York scroll thumbpiece. The exceptional and distinctive York acorn flagon has a bulbous lower section and

short spout. Examples are usually approximately 12in high.

A type of flagon made from about 1720 is the spire flagon. The body rests on a skirt base with a high domed cover and baluster finial. Handles are either a plain scroll with bold terminal or of broken scroll type. The smaller examples are classed as tankards. Variants of the style were made until the end of the 18th century.

Unlidded ale flagons or measures tend to be of rather more massive proportions than those previously mentioned

A beefeater flagon, showing "hallmarks" on the cover, inscribed "South Tawton 1685"; 10¾in.

A spire flagon, so named because of its finial, with "broken" handle, by Thomas Carpenter, c. 1760; 13in.

— of tapering cylindrical form, flared towards the base, and applied with a moulded girdle below the spout. On a smaller, more domestic, scale the ale or cider jugs or pitchers, made from the second half of the 18th century well into the 19th century, are rather more numerous. Most have chairback thumbpieces, although the one illustrated (p. 62), which is a fairly small example, has an attractive palmette thumbpiece. There are two body types: one bulbous with cylindrical neck, the other of slightly more graceful baluster form.

Left A fine example of an 18th-century cylindrical tankard, with engraved monogram at front, typical of the period; c. 1720, 7in.

Below left Three Bristol tulip-shaped tankards of the 18th century, showing variations in cover, thumbpiece and handle.

Below An 18th-century spouted ale flagon with the names of the owner and hostelry engraved; 11½in.

Three tankards of the Stuart period, two flat-topped (c. 1680) and one (c. 1695) with the later domed lid, engraved with wrigglework and with fretted denticulations at the lid-edges; 6¾, 7 and 6in.

TANKARDS

The styles of pewter tankards mirror those used by contemporary silversmiths. Tankards of the Stuart period are those most eagerly sought by collectors; they are the earliest type available and, in the opinion of the majority, the most attractive. Capacities were usually quart, 1½-pint or 1 pint (old English standard). They are of cylindrical form, with a moulded base and a stepped flat-topped cover. The scroll handle usually has a spade or volute terminal and there are a wide variety of thumbpieces. Many are charmingly engraved in the "wriggled" technique so popular at the time. Around 1700 the cover is sometimes pushed out into a high dome, heralding the Georgian dome-lidded tankards of 1720 onwards.

Eighteenth-century cylindrical tankards are usually encircled by a moulded girdle, the body gets thinner as the century progresses, the handle is an S-scroll. The handle terminals are one guide for dating, though not infallible: the spade or fishtail terminal generally gives way c. 1725 to the ball terminal, and by the end of the century the base of the handle is flush against the body – the type known as "attention". While 18th-century cylindrical tankards rarely have a double-scroll handle, this feature is found on later examples of tulip tankards and, around 1800 and later, on U-shaped tankards. The tulip, or baluster-shaped, tankards were made predominantly in the West Country, from around 1730, many by Bristol pewterers such as Allen Bright or Robert Bush.

BRITISH ISLES

MUGS

Pub mugs have great appeal to many people who do not consider themselves collectors or who would not normally use pewter for any other purpose. The pewter mug is part of the English tradition of ale and beer drinking, and while the beer drinker of the 1980s may not feel quite at home with a lidded tankard, he has no such problem when a mug is produced, thereby maintaining a tradition which stretches back 300 years and more. However, the majority of mugs seen in public houses and private homes today are post-Imperial (1826) mugs such as those described in this chapter being relatively scarce.

Surprisingly, whereas mugs of the 18th century in general reflect the styles of tankards, those of the 17th century do not. Mugs of 1670–1705 are of tapering form with a plain scroll or strap handle projecting from the lip. The body is usually circled with moulded bands. However, R. F. Michaelis in *British Pewter* illustrates an example in the Victoria and Albert Museum dated 1703 which is decorated with the lobing and fluting so popular at the time.

Early in the 18th century mugs become slightly squatter, with a moulded base and rather grander handle. By 1730–40 the handle had developed the ball terminal characteristic of the period, the cylindrical body resting on a tuck-in base. These styles continued to evolve throughout the century, with the introduction of the tulip-shape, then again the cylindrical; developments in the handle included the double-scroll, then the attention terminal as in tankards. The range of pub mugs from 1800 is shown on pp. 200 and 202.

MEASURES

To many collectors wine measures are the essence of English pewter. Their continental equivalents are the many regional measures of France or the measures of the Low

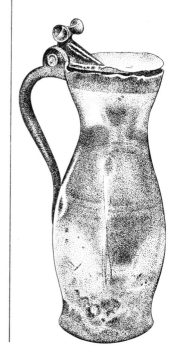

Left Pub mugs: tapering cylindrical, with WR mark at lip, c. 1700; tulip-shaped, of ½-pint capacity, also with WR mark, by Ingram and Hart, c. 1800; cylindrical, with side spout, by William Eddon, mid-18th century; cylindrical, with fishtail terminal, by Richard Going c. 1740 – 45; U-shaped, on "tuck-in" base, c. 1735 (this mug is stamped with WR and VR marks, showing that it was in use for over 100 years, see p. 240.)

Right Baluster wine measures, 18th-century; the one on the right has a "bud" thumbpiece.

Below right A baluster measure with double-volute thumbpiece; 18th century.

Below Two early English baluster wine measures showing the first types of thumbpiece used, hammer-head and ball.

Countries, with their gradually evolving styles. English wine measures are baluster-shaped, the form changing over the centuries from the elegant slender shape of the 16th century to the squatter 18th century type. As has already been mentioned, the body shape was most probably strongly influenced by early pottery. Baluster measures generally have a higher lead content in the alloy than most other English pewter.

Left A cider or ale jug, 1st half of the 19th century; 7½in high. This example has an attractive "palmette" thumbpiece; it is more usual to find these jugs with plain scroll or open chairback thumbpieces.

Above A Scottish measure of the type made in Edinburgh, with a flat-topped conical domed lid. The embryo shell thumbpiece is one of the most common on Scottish measures.

The most easily identifiable feature is the thumbpiece. The earliest forms of measure are those with the "hammerhead" and the "ball" thumbpiece, each of those being placed on the top of the wedge attachment to the lid. These types are extremely rare and date from the 16th to late 17th centuries. Easier to find today are the bud and double-volute measures, in sizes ranging from the gallon to the ½ gill. The extreme sizes are the most difficult to come by, the most common being the pint and ½-pint capacities. The bud measure was first known towards the end of the 17th century and it overlapped in the second quarter of the 18th century with the double-volute, which continued to be made for the rest of the century. In bud balusters there is a considerable variety in the incised lines round body and cover. Differences are also noticeable in handles: whereas the early types of measure have a simple handle attached directly to the body, the lower handle on some bud measures is separated from the body by a short strut. Some double-volutes maintain this feature, whilst others have a much bolder scroll handle with ball terminal.

Many measures have no maker's touch; others have only the excise mark; some early examples are stamped with a housemark, usually on the lid.

One regional type of measure of a quite different style is the West Country spirit measure. These measures are of bulbous form, tapering to a narrow neck before flaring out at the lip in the shape of an inverted cone. The bulge at the base either tucks in to a spreading foot or rests on simple moulding. The latter type could be confused with the Irish "haystack" measure (see below).

SCOTLAND

Nearly all Scottish baluster measures are 19th-century and they are very similar to those made in England. The two most common forms of thumbpiece are the ball and the embryo-shell. The former must not be confused with the rare early English type – always chec' the style of the body and the wedge joining cover and ball. Apart from these measures, the two chief centres of Scottish pewterers, Edinburgh and Glasgow, each have distinctive measures.

Tappit-hens in Scottish one pint (late 18th century), and Chopin and Mutchkin (c. 1800) capacities; 11, 9 and 6¾in. (See p. 65 also.)

Right A West Country spirit measure, not to be confused with the Irish "Haystack" measure. The handle shows how pewter sometimes flakes under certain conditions.

Far right A Glasgow measure of Imperial pint capacity.

The curve of the body line is more pronounced and the covers are completely different, that from Glasgow being a gently rounded curve, the Edinburgh type a more conical dome, flat in the centre. As well as the maker's mark, often struck (or cast, see p. 236) inside the cover, these measures often have capacity seals (also sometimes cast on the lid) and Dean of Guild marks.

The best known piece of Scottish pewter is undoubtedly the tappit-hen – either plain or crested (i.e. with finial). They were principally made in three sizes: Scots pint (equal to three Imperial pints), chopin (1½ Imperial pints) and mutchkin (¾ Imperial pint), although the full range is much wider. Some have a plouk inside the body for measuring the true capacity. Tappit-hens were made throughout the 18th century and until about 1850.

The earlier pot-belly measure shows most clearly Scotland's connections with the Low Countries. Compare this shape with that of the Rembrandtkan on p. 148. The thumbpiece of a pot-belly measure or a tappit-hen is also very similar to that of Dutch measures.

Except for the rare pot-belly measures, the great majority of extant Scottish pewter post-dates the 1745 rebellion, when Bonnie Prince Charlie failed to regain the throne for the Stuarts. Very little ecclesiastical pewter survives from before that date and the majority of 18th- and early 19th-century flagons were made for ecclesiastical use. Scottish flagons are of tapering cylindrical outline with a central

Opposite, left A Scottish pot-bellied measure; early 18th century. These also occur in unlidded form. The affinity with the Rembrandtkan of the Low Countries is apparent (see p. 148). *Centre* A Scottish "thistle" measure of one pint (post Imperial) capacity. These were made in a range of sizes but are now rare; their shape held back part of the due measure. *Right* A Scottish crested tappit-hen, 18th/early 19th century. Both this and the type lacking a finial (see p. 63) were made in various capacities, the largest about 12in high.

Scottish communion pewter inscribed "Associate Congrn. Lanark" and dated 1791; chalices 8in; flagons, by James Wright of Edinburgh, 10½in.

Below A mid-18th-century Irish flagon; 12in. Note the bold scrolling of the handle. The spreading foot, short spout and flat-topped domed cover are also characteristic.

moulded girdle and reeding at the base; some have spouts. The flat cover has a bifurcated thumbpiece; some covers have a finial. The flagons are usually engraved with the name of the kirk, as are the accompanying communion cups and basins. Communion tokens were issued to those who wished to receive the sacrament; they usually have the name of the parish on one side, with perhaps a suitable biblical reference on the reverse.

IRELAND

The main centres of pewter making in Ireland were Dublin and Cork, although Charles Clarke of Waterford was a fairly prolific maker of flatware around 1800. The Irish were as troubled as the English by "counterfeit" pewter and the local trade was also deeply affected by the large quantity of imported wares. England was not the only source of the imports, and the competition was not only in the form of pewter – Cotterell quotes from the Irish House of Commons *Journal* of 1753: "Petition of the manufacturers of block-tin in Ireland, stating that owing to the great importation of Rouen, Burgundy and Marseilles earthenware, the trade of pewterers is at a standstill."

Ecclesiastical vessels form an important part of known Irish pewter. Chalices usually have straight-sided bowls which rest on thick cylindrical stems. The most noticeable feature of Irish flagons is the extravagantly scrolling handle. The cylindrical body usually has a short spout and rests on a

Irish Haystack or Harvester measures, by Austen of Cork, 19th century; 3¾in, 5in and 6in.

rounded spreading base. The domed cover usually has a volute thumbpiece.

A popular form of 19th-century Irish measure is the harvester or haystack measure, which ranges from ½-gill to gallon capacities. As in the English West Country measures, the lip is of inverted cone form. The body flares out from the narrow neck to a moulded girdle at the shoulder, from which the line continues straight down to the moulded base. Many harvester measures were made by Joseph Austen and Son of Cork and their successors the Munster Iron Company, and bear their marks on the underside. There are also many modern reproductions.

Another range of Irish measures, made in four small sizes, is the baluster measure. These have no handles and are often stamped with the capacity on the body.

The largest (half pint) and smallest (quarter gill) of the range of four Irish baluster measures. Only the smallest is of the concave-sided shape.

CHANNEL ISLANDS

Pewter making was concentrated on the largest islands, Guernsey and Jersey. In spite of their proximity to France, Channel Islands pewterers maintained close connections with England, and often stamped their work "London" in the same way that was popular with provincial pewterers.

Not surprisingly, there is obvious French influence in the style of the local measures, specifically the heart-shaped cover and twin-acorn thumbpiece, features which do not appear elsewhere in the British Isles. Jersey flagons are of plain baluster form, the body ending flush with the base. The Guernsey type is rather more elegant, the slender pear-shaped body resting on a spreading foot and often enlivened with girdles round neck and belly. Capacities range from pot (2 quarts) to ½ noggin, they include six sizes in Jersey but fewer in Guernsey. Many Channel Islands measures bear capacity stamps.

A Guernsey measure, by
Joseph Wingod, mid-18th
century; 11½in.

A Jersey measure, by J. de St
Croix, 18th century; 10¾in.

FRANCE

It is not far across the Gulf of St Malo from the Channel Islands to France and there are obvious similarities between the flagons of Guernsey and Jersey and those of Normandy. The connection is shown in the unusual Normandy measure illustrated (p. 76), which was made for export and bears Guernsey excise marks. As in other parts of the continent, in France the design of measures is based on regional forms. There are areas of the country, particularly central France, where pewterers (other than local tinkers) do not appear to have worked, but Tardy in *Les Étains français* lists 500 places where pewter was made. There is a higher proportion of provincial than Parisian pewter available today, as much pewter was melted down in the capital for re-use. There are certain towns of notable importance, Paris, Lyon and Bordeaux in particular, and there are two border areas with which we should be primarily concerned, the north, where the main centre was Lille, and the eastern border along the Rhine.

The only major changes in the boundaries of France since the death of Louis XIV in 1715 (excluding the years of Napoleon) came in 1860 with the ceding of Savoy and Nice to France. Alsace and Lorraine, major acquisitions of the 17th and 18th centuries, remained French until the end of the Franco-Prussian war in 1871, when they were handed to Germany; they finally reverted to France after World War I. Pewter made in this area along the Rhine has in many respects a closer affinity to Germany than to France. Likewise, Flemish pewter takes little account of present borders – northeast France, for example, witnessed the battles of the 17th and 18th centuries which resulted from the power struggle between the major kingdoms of Europe.

In the 13th century Henry II of England ruled more territory than did the King of France, but by the end of the Hundred Years War in 1453 there was some degree of unity in France and the beginnings of centralized government for the first time since Charlemagne. This was consolidated in the late 15th and early 16th centuries but the Reformation threatened to divide the country once more and religious dissension halted economic expansion. John Calvin founded the first French Protestant church in Strasbourg in 1538, and French adherents of Calvinism came to be known as Huguenots.

RELIEF PEWTER, THE HUGUENOTS, LOUIS XIV

One victim of the early persecution of Huguenots was François Briot, perhaps the most famous of all pewterers. Born in Damblain in Lorraine in about 1550, he was forced to flee to Montbéliard in 1579. Here he became a medallist to the Duke of Württemberg. Although the first documented master to have made relief pewter in France was Roland Greffet of Lyon (1528–68), it was Briot who developed the

The chief pewter-making centres of France. Different styles of, for example, wine measure were produced in different regions which often straddled shifting frontiers – Lille and Flanders, Strasbourg and the Rhineland, the Swiss border areas and the Channel Islands providing examples.

ENGLAND

Dunquerque FLANDERS
Calais St Ormer BELGIUM
Boulogne Lille
ARTOIS
Arras

ENGLISH CHANNEL
Dieppe Amiens
Neufchâtel PICARDY
Rouen Reims

GERMANY

Guernsey
CHANNEL
ISLANDS Jersey
Caen NORMANDY
Falaise
Versailles
ISLE DE
FRANCE
Paris
CHAMPAGNE

Metz
LORRAINE
Nancy Strasbourg
ALSACE
Colmar
Mulhouse

Chartres
MAINE
Troyes
Montbéliard

BRITTANY Rennes Le Mans
ORLÉANS

ANJOU
Angers
Tours
TOURRAINE
BERRY

Dijon
BURGUNDY
NIVERNAIS
Besançon
FRANCHE COMTÉ
SWITZERLAND

Nantes

POITOU
BORBONNAIS

La Rochelle
LA MARCHE
Limoges
LIMOUSIN
Clermont-Ferrand
AUVERGNE

SAVOY

Lyon

BAY OF BISCAY

Bordeaux
Dordogne
GUYENNE
Garonne

GASCONY
Toulouse

NAVARRE

DAUPHINÉ ITALY

NICE

LANGUEDOC PROVENCE
Aix
Marseille

SPAIN

Ebro

MEDITERRANEAN SEA

Rhine
Meuse
Seine
Loire
Rhône

frontier in 1660
frontier in 1789
present-day frontier

0   100mi
0   150km

The "Temperentia" dish (1585–90) by François Briot, 17¾in. Briot made an accompanying ewer, but the ewer illustrated should accompany his similar creation, the Mars dish.

technique and so brought his craft to heights of artistic excellence never before achieved in pewter. Influenced by the mannerist style of the School of Fontainebleau, today known principally through engravings, Briot created the "Temperantia" dish (1585–90). In the centre is a seated woman, an allegorical figure of Temperance, surrounded by the four elements, earth, fire, air and water, and, on the rim, the seven liberal arts, amid fruit and various grotesques. The accompanying ewer bears figures of Faith, Hope and Charity. Briot's Temperantia dish was copied and modified many times in pewter, silver and enamel by a number of artists. One of the best known versions is probably the Ladies Trophy of the Wimbledon Lawn Tennis Championships, a modern silver-gilt electrotype of Caspar Enderlein's version of Briot's Temperantia dish now in the Louvre. Briot made another model for a ewer and dish in the same vein, the dish centred by Mars. He used his moulds well into the 17th century, and after his death about 1616 they came into the hands of Isaac Faust of Strasbourg, who cast pieces from them which he stamped with his own mark. Faust also made relief pewter to his own designs, notably tankards (see p. 28), maintaining the high standard of craftsmanship set by Briot. Briot and Faust established a tradition in France for the making of fine quality pewter and earned French pewter a high reputation which was never lost. Relief pewter continued to be popular in Strasbourg until the early 18th century, particularly fine workmanship being executed on écuelles.

Unfortunately very little French pewter survives which was made before the mid-17th century other than relief pewter. Among the few pieces that do exist are gothic faceted and cimarre flagons, both mentioned with other early pieces in the Introduction (pp. 17, 22).

During the long reign of Louis XIV (1643–1715) the political and social influence of France blossomed. Literature, drama, architecture, etiquette, philosophy – all reached peaks of excellence and refinement at a time when on a battlefield it seemed as though France was invincible. However, in 1685, influenced by a surge of piety and an increasing desire for uniformity, Louis revoked the Edict of Nantes, which had given Huguenots full civic rights and freedom of public worship. The result was an exodus of Huguenots – an estimated 400,000 people, chiefly from the prosperous and hard-working middle classes. They took with them their talents for industry and trade, to the enormous benefit of the countries in which they settled, principally the Netherlands, England and Germany. The skills of Huguenot craftsmen transformed the quality and style of goldsmiths' work in these countries, which was reflected in that of pewterers. The cost of war had also exhausted France's economic resources. Heavy taxes were imposed, the use of silver for domestic purposes severely restricted and large quantities of plate were requisitioned to replenish the national coffers. Not even the king was exempt, and in 1689 the silver furniture in the palace of Versailles was melted down. In 1709 there was a further crisis in the national finances and members of the court were again expected to surrender their silver. The folly and shortsightedness of this plan was realized at the time – it was after all but a drop in the ocean – ahd the reluctance of the aristocracy to comply is recorded by the Duc de Saint-Simon in his memoirs of court life: "Some people had clung to their silver plates as a last resource and dreaded to part with them; others feared the dirtiness of pewter and earthenware. . . All the nobility took to eating off porcelain within a week with the result that the china shops were emptied and prices rose sky high" (*The Historical Memoirs of the Duc de Saint-Simon*, ed. L. Norton, 1968–74). However, not everyone was as fastidious as Saint-Simon. When they could not have silver, people turned to pewter and the result was a tremendous boost in the

Above Wine tasters with flat, plain ring, and entwined snake handles.

Left A pair of candlesticks, of faceted baluster form; the stems unscrew at the join with the high domed bases; mid-18th century, 10¼in.

Above Gadrooning and strap-work on a beaker of Louis xiv's reign.

Above right A tureen, by Antoine Joseph of Strasbourg; c. 1800, 10in diameter.

fortunes of the trade. Pewterers took over much of the work of silversmiths in the making of tableware, adopting their designs and enlarging the range of items made.

DOMESTIC PEWTER

The importance of French domestic pewter of Louis xiv's reign lies in its quality and variety – stylistically to a very large extent it simply mirrored contemporary silver. Mustard pots, salt cellars, candlesticks, spoons, beakers, wine tasters, casters and cruets all had the features which made French silver and silversmiths so highly respected. Pieces with octagonal or bell-shaped outlines had borders of gadrooning and entwined strapwork and were further decorated with well-executed piercing and engraving. None of this had previously featured in the pewterer's oeuvre.

The increased use of pewter, which had begun in times of emergency, continued despite the ever-growing popularity of faience. For most of the 18th century a large proportion of households would have possessed a reasonable quantity of pewter. During Louis xv's decadent reign domestic pewter continued to be made, reflecting the changes in taste. In the 1730s and 1740s pewter was still being made in which clarity of line and proportion were of paramount importance, although the influence of rococo on the traditional French classical form is clearly seen, for example on candlesticks and tureens. Strasbourg, due to its proximity to Germany, was the chief exponent of rococo in household pewter. In the second half of the 18th century, as porcelain and earthenware became cheaper through the development of local factories and imports from Holland and England, their popularity spread down the social scale: pewterers struggled to compete by producing coffee pots, candlesticks and other requisites in styles then in vogue, but it was a doomed trade.

FRANCE

After the Revolution of 1789, under the influence of Napoleon and the confidence which his government inspired, the arts flourished once more. There was a brief revival in the fortunes of the pewterer's trade. In the late 18th and the early 19th centuries pieces were made in the neo-classical and Empire styles. Coffee pots and milk jugs are among the items from this period most readily available to the modern collector. Another household item which continued to be popular into the 19th century is the soup tureen. In less wealthy homes a plain, practical form was preferred and these continued to be made for the rest of the century. Around 1800 the firm lines of neo-classicism introduced a new dimension and we find suites of tureens and vegetable dishes in varying sizes. The bodies and covers of these pieces in the early 19th century were usually plain, decoration being limited to handles, borders and finials.

JUGS, PITCHERS AND EWERS

Ewers (aiguières) were an item on which particular care was lavished. The term applies not only to the relief ewers of the late 16th century but also to the helmet-shaped ewer which was most popular from about 1680 to 1720. There are two main body types: those which have a bell-shaped body and a short spout (these sometimes have a hinged cover), and the helmet-shaped type, where the pouring lip is integrated into the curve of the rim (this style is compared to a Greek soldier's inverted helmet). In both types the body rests on a domed spreading foot and there is a harp-shaped handle. Decorative detail varies according to date and region; nearly all have moulded girdles, some have gadroon borders to the foot or applied strapwork at the base of the body.

The water jug (pot à l'eau) is far less graceful than the helmet-shaped ewer but has a sturdy character of its own. It has a bulbous body below a cylindrical neck and rests on a domed foot. The scroll handle often has applied beading. These jugs were initially used for water for washing hands but they continued to be made as vessels for carrying water throughout the 18th and into the 19th century, with minor stylistic changes.

A characteristically Parisian vessel is the broc à vin. These wine jugs were made in various sizes, some quite large, mostly in the 19th century but also in the 18th. The body tapers outwards down to the belly and then narrows towards the foot; it is usually encircled by many moulded or engraved bands. The loop handle is usually ridged on the inside to help the grip. Some examples have a detachable stopper. A 19th-century development of this broc à vin has a slanting cover and erect thumbpiece.

One other vessel should briefly be mentioned here, which is for oil, in French a mesure à huile. These measures are

Above Two ewers (*aiguières*), c. 1680–1700; 11in and 9½in.

Right A 19th-century water jug, 7in.

Left Broc à vin (wine pitcher); 19th century, 15¼in. This example is missing its stopper.

usually baluster-shaped with very narrow faceted or cylindrical spouts (also seen on the *cruche à lait*, see Food Containers below), but the design varies depending on date and origin.

MEASURES

French wine measures (*pichets*) fall into three main shapes: shouldered, baluster and the less popular tapering cylindrical. All have covers and some sort of spout or shaped lip for pouring. The majority of pichets found today are 18th-century. The cylindrical type, being of stitzen form, is restricted almost entirely to the Rhine borders, principally in the province of Alsace. The other two types intermingle, with the exception of the baluster flagons of Flanders. In his study *Les Pichets d'étain* M. Charles Boucaud includes a map showing the major areas for each type. There is a broad band in the north from Normandy to Lorraine densely marked with towns where measures were made, but south of the Loire there are only isolated centres: Bordeaux, Clermont-Ferrand and a cluster on the Mediterranean in southern Languedoc and Provence. These pieces did not derive from a central source – each area developed its own characteristic measure. It is not possible to discuss here at length all the minutiae of regional differences in the various measures, but the following should serve to identify the principal types.

Above An 18th-century oil measure *(mesure à huile)*.

Left Two Normandy measures. *Left* An unlidded version of the type shown on p. 79; this one bears Channel Island marks. *Right* Falaise type, quart capacity; 1st half 19th century, 9½in. Note the similarity in cover shape and thumbpiece (twin acorn) with the lidded Normandy measure.

Right Three provincial
measures, or *pichets*, of
shouldered form, from (*left*)
Picardy; (*centre*) Joinville and
(*right*) Troyes, both in
Champagne.

Right Three provincial
measures, or *pichets*, of
shouldered form, from (*left*)
Picardy; (*centre*) Joinville and
(*right*) Troyes, both in
Champagne.

Regional types of measure,
left to right Orléans, 5¼in;
Chartres, 5¾in, Toulouse,
dated 1709 in the touch,
9¼in.

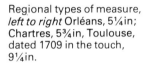

Paris, naturally, was an important centre. The pichets made here are of shouldered type, the body resting on an almost vertical foot rim. It has a simple scroll handle and flat heart-shaped cover with an erect thumbpiece, which is usually ridged. The foot and thumbpiece are the most distinctive features on Parisian measures. This shape developed from the spoutless measures of the 17th century, the chief difference being the cover: in the earlier type this was circular, of domed tapering form with a wedge or twin-acorn thumbpiece.

The pichets of Paris and those made in its environs have elegant, slender proportions. Once outside the capital the measures become rather more bulky, particularly in Normandy, where shouldered flagons were made in large numbers well into the 19th century. These Normandy flagons have a practical and rather ungainly air. The thumbpiece here is always twin-acorn and the lower part of the

Left A measure of the type made in Paris; by Nicholas Marchand of Versailles; c. 1730, 9in.

Regional types of measure, *left to right*: Toulouse, 17th century, 6¾in; Clermont-Ferrand (Auvergne), late 18th century, 9¼in; Anjou or Maine, 18th century; Normandy, 18th or early 19th century.

body flares outwards right at the bottom to form a base. There is seldom any banding on the body. The majority are approximately 10in high, or of pot capacity, although the range of smaller quart and pint sizes were made. Quite often the owner's name or initials were engraved down the handle-back, or initials stamped on the lid.

Also in Normandy, specifically in and around the town of Falaise, was made a slender form of baluster measure. The long neck is circled by engraved bands which are repeated on the bulging body; the foot is flared; the flat heart-shaped cover has a twin-acorn thumbpiece.

Baluster and shouldered pichets made in Orléans have a feature peculiar to that area. The high cylindrical collar is cut off at a slant towards the hinge (a feature seen on the broc à vin) and the lid falls inside the collar.

FRANCE

North-eastern measure, by Lefebre of Lille; 1st half 19th century, 8in. Similar measures were made across the border in the Low Countries.

In Champagne, they made an elongated form of shouldered flagon, with a variant in Joinville, and Picardy is another province with very distinctive styles, the cylindrical body of the measure widening quite low down its length, with a heart-shaped cover.

Other types of measure are found throughout the northern half of the country, with slight variations in outline and different thumbpieces. For example in Anjou an attractive palmette thumbpiece was used. Some shouldered flagons, especially those made in Bordeaux and in the southern districts, have a similar outline to the Swiss kelchkanne.

In the northeast (Lille, St Omer, Valenciennes), we find a completely different type of baluster or pear-shaped measure. They are very similar to Low Countries measures – perhaps slightly squatter – and the shallow domed covers have either erect or shell thumbpieces. There is usually also a short spout.

METRIC MEASURES
In 1795 the metric system was introduced. This important change produced a completely new type of cylindrical measure which the modern collector should find quite

A 19th-century metric measure of double-litre capacity, 10in. These measures were made in a range of sizes and also with the lid falling outside the collar, or without a lid *(see drawings)*. (Compare with measures made in the Low Countries, p. 151).

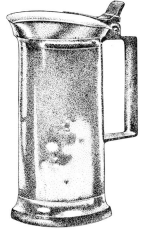

frequently. They were made in sizes ranging from 2-litre down to centilitre (approx. 10in to 2in), throughout the 19th and into the 20th century. A large number seem to have been made in Lille by makers such as Humbert Leclerc or Legrand. Cylindrical measures were also made in the Low Countries. Paris was a large manufacturer, but of course they were produced in numerous other centres as well. There are three main types: lidless, those with a lid which falls inside the collar, and those where the lid falls outside. The last two types have erect thumbpieces; all have an angular handle. The size is often engraved at the front and they are often covered by inspectors' stamps round the lip. The maker's mark is stamped on the base. (French measures have verification stamps in the Roman alphabet, Flemish in the Greek.)

STRASBOURG MEASURES AND FLAGONS
The vessels made in Strasbourg for carrying wine were, as has already been explained, far more similar to German flagons than French pichets. This also applies to other centres along the Rhine such as Colmar. The most common flagon is of tapering cylindrical or "stitze" form, the body encircled by several moulded and engraved bands. The

A flagon by Leonard Wehrlen of Strasbourg, marked on the handle and dated 1725 at front; early 18th century, 14in.

A measure from Picardy, 9½in.

scroll handle usually has a simple ridged terminal and is surmounted by an erect thumbpiece. Variations are found in the cover and spout: when there is only a small projection to pour from the cover is usually flat and heart-shaped.

Another form has a bold beak-like spout (also found in Germany, Austria and Switzerland); this is combined with a moulded domed cover, centred by a tiered finial and with a projection covering the spout. This combination of spout and domed cover is found too on bulbous-shaped flagons with a high spreading foot, also made in Strasbourg, which have close similarities to flagons made in Germany, e.g. in Frankfurt and Stuttgart. These were sometimes adapted for ecclesiastical use, and have an Agnus Dei thumbpiece.

ÉCUELLES

Strasbourg was a centre for the making of écuelles, as has been previously mentioned. Other centres were Bordeaux, Paris, Rouen and Lyon. The écuelle's basic shape and size (some 6in in diameter) altered very little, but craftsmen lavished an enormous amount of care and attention on the decorative details. All have a shallow circular body with two flat "ears" or handles, and if there is a cover it is domed with a central finial. Écuelles were first made in the mid-17th

century and reached the height of their popularity 1670 – 1740. However they continued to be made in the rococo style in the second half of the 18th century, and well into the 19th century for use in hospitals. Many early examples are lidless, although they most probably did once have a cover which has been lost. The main areas for decoration were the lid and ears – the latter were often shaped and pierced. During Louis xiv's reign the contemporary decorative motifs were used: gadroon and beaded borders, lobing and strapwork and palmettes on the ears; all these being cast or applied. Relief decoration, incorporating arabesques, motifs of marriage, allegorical figures and flowers, remained popular on écuelles until about 1740. By this time écuelles were no longer being made in Paris in large quantities and Lyon had become a major centre. Bordeaux favoured the rococo style and continued to use it on écuelles until the early 19th century – long after it had ceased to be fashionable elsewhere.

DISHES AND PLATES
Mid-17th century dishes were similar to those of other countries and particularly popular was the "cardinal's hat" type. The broad plain rim was usually engraved with armorials and the marks, too, were stamped on the front. Large broad-rimmed dishes of 22in or 24in were also made for serving meat. This design was mostly made between 1640 and 1670 but continued into the 18th century. Under the influence of silversmiths at the end of the 17th century, the borders of plates generally became narrower and marks were stamped on the reverse of the rim. From 1675 to 1700 gadrooning or beading decorated the edges. Moulded and reeded borders also became fashionable around 1680–1700. Another development was the curved rim, which is found on

Two early 18th-century *écuelles* and covers; 10½ and 11in.

84

plates of varying sizes and also on oval dishes – a new shape. These plates became immensely popular and continued to be made long into the 19th century. The wavy-edged plate was introduced around 1730. Also made at this time was the very attractive dish known in England as the "strawberry dish". The raised sides are fluted into sections, sometimes as many as thirty-two. Some examples have an everted scalloped border with a beaded or gadroon edge. These strawberry dishes are often centred by engraved armorials or initials, whereas most plates have such engraving on the border, where it is not so easily damaged by knife scratches.

The making of plates was not confined to any particular area: they were made in large quantities in the provinces where the size of the plates, as well as the decoration, varied from place to place. In Strasbourg, particularly, the engraving of scenes on plates was a popular form of decoration which produced enormous variety. The French were adventurous in designing their plates – far more so than the English, who rather grudgingly made a small quantity of decorative plates of very fine quality but who never really accepted the continental fashions.

FOOD CONTAINERS

Travellers like to carry refreshments with them and people working on the land also need to have food brought to them for eating out in the fields. Various containers were used for this purpose and others were made for use in the house, in many different shapes and sizes. And so there is the *pot à beurre* (for butter), the *porte-dîner* (for solid food), the *farinière* (for flour), the *cruche à lait* (for milk), the *pot à consommé* (for soup) and the *bouteille* (for wine). All are objects found more frequently in France than elsewhere. The main characteristic of containers used outside the house is a swing carrying handle and a closely fitting cover – in the case of the *cruche à lait* these are usually hinged. The baluster vessels for liquid have screw tops. The *bouteille* developed from the pear-shaped pilgrim bottles, and similar examples are found in most countries in both pewter and silver. Originally slung by their chains on carriages, they evolved a flattened form which was more comfortable to attach to a belt or shoulder strap. The quality, size and decoration of these *bouteilles* varies greatly: a few were made for display only.

CISTERNS

In eastern France, German and Swiss traditions influenced the making of water cisterns with accompanying basins. These are described in the chapters on those two countries and it is usually only the marks which distinguish French examples.

Below A bottle for water or wine with close-fitting screw top and swing carrying-handle – two indications of its out-door use.

Bottom A flour container (*farinière*), one of a number of food containers in pewter whose manufacture was more common in France than elsewhere.

CHURCH PEWTER

A considerable quantity of religious pewter was made in France. Crucifixes, plaques and busts of the Holy Family and saints were made to hang in the home as well as in churches. Holy water stoups (*bénitiers*) are also found in varied forms, the majority of which hung on the wall backed by relief plaquettes. Church furnishings such as altar candlesticks, sanctuary lamps and chalices were, of course, made in pewter. Some of the most attractive pieces of church pewter are altar cruets (*burettes*). A very popular form from the 18th century is of simple baluster shape, on spreading base, with either plain or helmet-shaped neck. They stand on a tray, which is usually oval. Other burettes were contained in rectangular caskets; when these caskets contain three cylindrical vessels (the third being for holy oil) they are termed chrismatories – used for giving the last rites, the sacrament of Extreme Unction. Early chrismatories are plain, with domed lids surmounted frequently by a cross finial. The cover often has a clasp at the front very similar to the hinge, although the pin for this clasp has usually been lost. In the 18th century the casket is sometimes decorated with gadroon and foliate borders.

Left Cruche à lait with fixed handle, marked on the hinged lid by Pissavy of Lyon; 19th century, 12½in.

Right A *porte-dîner* with swing handle; 2nd half 18th century, 7in.

GERMANY AND AUSTRIA – HUNGARY

Central Europe, including those parts that we know today as Germany, Austria, Poland, Czechoslovakia, Hungary and northern Italy, has a complex history of many diverse peoples developing individually and yet linked by political, religious, social and artistic ties which caused them to form and reform in constantly changing alliances. For most of its history Germany had no capital – no one place where the arts, literature and philosophy flourished. Instead all the cities and states developed their own identities and cultures. Only in Vienna was there a political as well as an artistic centre and Vienna in the 18th century became a truly cosmopolitan city. Like Paris, it was an important centre for pewterers but little of their work is available today, as much of it was melted for re-use.

The chief pewter-making centres in German-speaking and neighbouring areas. The Holy Roman Empire, of which the frontiers of the Treaty of Westphalia are indicated, was not dissolved until 1806.

The heart of this vast area was the Holy Roman Empire, which consisted of a mass of small self-governing states whose leaders came to have titles such as king, duke, prince, margrave, elector. All owed allegiance to the emperor, who was the secular leader of western Christendom, crowned by the Pope. In the 13th century several northern cities, including Lübeck, Hamburg and Bremen, formed the Hanseatic League to aid commerce (see introduction p. 16) and in the south Augsburg and Nuremberg became the principal artistic centres. There was great movement amongst the population as craftsmen travelled from one city to another and colonists moved eastwards.

By the end of the 15th century the two families who were to dominate the later history of Germany were firmly established: in the southeast the Hapsburgs owned Austria and provided the empire with its rulers, and in the north the Hohenzollerns ruled Brandenburg and Prussia. By the mid-16th century the Hapsburgs had acquired the Netherlands, Burgundy, Spain, Italy and Hungary. But the Reformation was spreading, particularly in the north, and the importance of empire was beginning to dwindle as individual states became stronger. By the 1648 Treaty of Westphalia which ended the Thirty Years War, Germany was fragmented – there were 350 units of government, the largest of which were Prussia and Austria. When Louis xiv revoked the Edict of Nantes, 20,000 French Huguenots fled to Protestant Prussia, where their skills did much to help that state's rapid expansion. Throughout the 18th century, under rulers such as Maria Theresa of Austria and Frederick the Great of Prussia, the power of these two states increased; but others should not be ignored, such as Brunswick and Hanover, whose elector was also king of England. By the time the Holy Roman Empire was finally dissolved in 1806, Poland had been partitioned between Austria, Prussia and Russia, and Napoleon had conquered the continent and reorganized Germany. In the 19th century the empires of Prussia and Austria-Hungary recovered their fortunes, helped by their respective ministers, Bismarck and Metternich, and the idea of Germany as a nation began to emerge.

From the Middle Ages a major source of tin for pewterers throughout the empire were the mines in the Erzgebirge (or Ore Mountains) in Saxony; tin was also mined in Bohemia. In the late 17th and the 18th centuries production was stepped up to meet the increased demand for domestic pewterware. The present output from these mines is small.

GUILD PEWTER

A large proportion of the guild pewter still in existence is German and the German trade guilds had greater power than those of any other country with the possible exception

RUSSIA

MOLDAVIA

TRANSYLVANIA

Sighişoara●
(Schässburg)

sent-day nation-states and their borders
ntier of the Holy Roman Empire in 1648

0 ————————— 200mi

0 ————————— 300km

Two rooms from a dolls' house made in Nuremberg in 1673. Many of the pewter items bear the touches of Nuremberg pewterers. The dishes are an average of 2in in diameter, the flagons about 3in tall, and the rooms 15in high.

Pewter in a large and busy kitchen of the early 18th century; from a 1715 Nuremberg edition of Giovanni Battista della Porta, *Magia Naturalis*.

of England. The guilds dominated the lives of their members from the moment they entered apprenticeship, and every practice in a member's craft was governed by the rules and traditions of his guild. In the 15th and 16th centuries German guilds encouraged their apprentices to travel and gain experience of other cultures; many did not return, but spread their inherited traditions to their adopted home.

The outstanding corporation and guild pewter of the late 15th to mid-17th centuries has been discussed in the Introduction (pp. 20–27). In the late 17th and the 18th centuries – indeed also in the 19th century – pewter made for guilds, or pewter with relevant inscriptions, was not of such massive size as the earlier pieces, due to changes in customs and table habits. The items most usually found are tankards or flagons, and cups; plates are less common. They are invariably of good quality and bear an inscription which might include the relevant guild or similar body, the names of the master, members, donor or recipient and dates – or, quite simply, the owner's name. There is often also an emblem, for example a loaf of bread for bakers; trowel, mallet and rule for mason and bricklayers; a bull or meat cleaver for butchers; a shoe for bootmakers.

The covered cups rest on a knopped pedestal foot; the body has a cylindrical section between moulded bands at the lip and base, onto which are often applied lion's masks, from which hang variously engraved tokens. The detachable domed cover has a figure finial usually of military nature, holding a banner and shield. The actual shape of the cups varies considerably within these broad guidelines, and many cups have by now lost their tokens, shield and banner – sometimes also the finial.

RELIEF PEWTER (EDELZINN)

Although relief pewter was first made in France and its greatest exponent, François Briot, was French, it is in Germany that we find the most numerous and prolific craftsmen in this genre. The main centre for German *Edelzinn* was Nuremberg, but it was made in other centres throughout the empire, including even Italy. Families of pewterers worked in the same tradition, and one generation would use its predecessors' moulds. Sometimes the actual engraving of the mould, in intaglio, was done by a professional engraver rather than the pewterer and all borrowed from the designs of ornament engravers, which freely circulated among

A plate of the bakers' guild, by Daniel Gottlob Reinhard of Zittau, dated 1800; 9¾in.

craftsmen of the day – goldsmiths, cabinet makers and pewterers alike. The most popular items for *Edelzinn* were dishes, plates and tankards, but cups, porringers, flasks, flagons and salts were also made.

François Briot's most renowned follower was Caspar Enderlein, whose Temperantia dish, a copy of that of his master, has already been mentioned (p. 71). Enderlein was born in Basel in 1560 and in 1583–4 settled in Nuremberg, where he lived until his death in 1633. His best moulds date from about 1610–25. Both he and Isaac Faust of Strasbourg (1606–69) made very similar tankards of tapering cylindrical form, the body divided into panels centred by female figures, most probably copied from Briot's Mars dish. On Enderlein's tankard the figures represent America, Africa and Europe, but on Faust's they represent Patienta (patience, endurance) and Solertia (skillfulness, expertise). Faust's tankard has a caryatid handle, while Enderlein's has one of scroll form. Enderlein's moulds were used by another Nuremberg pewterer, Jacob Koch II (1572–1619), who made several other fine pieces of relief pewter. Similar tankards were also made by Melchior Horcheimer, who was working in Nuremberg around 1600.

In the previous generation, Nicholas Horcheimer made fine relief dishes. M. Charles Boucaud compares the texture of his work to that of wood engraving: the borders of his dishes and those of his school have a completely different style and feeling from the work of the craftsmen previously mentioned. The relief work is flatter; the elongated figures are clustered together in mannerist poses in a close-knit

Above Two 17th-century plates in relief. *Left* Depicting Christ and the Apostles. *Right* A Kaiserteller, the central medallion depicting Ferdinand III (1608–57), by Ulrich Appel, both 7in.

Right "Edelzinn". Detail from a tankard by Jobst Sigmund of Nuremberg in imitation of the style of Caspar Enderlein; late 17th century.

composition which makes less use of cartouches than the later masters.

The size of 16th-century "display" dishes varies from about 6in to 18in. The broad rims were usually decorated with strapwork, foliage, figures or animals and the raised central boss had allegorical figures. In the 17th century borders narrowed slightly and parts of the dish were sometimes left quite plain. Also in this century a group of commemorative plates (German: *Teller*) were made, many by a father and son bearing the same name, Paulus Oham. The *Kaiserteller* is centred by Ferdinand III on horseback, and the rim is decorated with the Electors. Other plates were made commemorating Ferdinand II and Gustavus Adolphus, while others of a biblical nature depict Christ Risen, the Prophets, Adam and Eve, or Noah's sacrifice. Usually 7–9 in in diameter, these plates continued to be made into the early 18th century. Modern collectors should keep an eye open for late casts, and for the many reproductions that are made of these plates (they are usually of a heavy gauge of metal and have a rather coarse texture whereas 17th-century examples are light and soft). Differences can also be seen in the turning on the reverse of the plates, early examples being turned in a spiral, later ones in concentric circles. The later casts, taken from the originals, contain the maker's touch in the casting instead of having this stamped on completion of the piece.

Relief pewter made outside Nuremberg in the mid-16th century is sometimes of heavier and thicker design, but is nevertheless of fine quality. There was a strong preference for tankards – decorated in horizontal bands encircling the body, frequently with biblical scenes and figures enclosed within arches, as in a freize. Joachimsthal, a town close to the mines in Saxony, was one centre for this type of tankard. Towards the end of the 17th century, the baroque style was used; plates had borders of boldly modelled fruit and flowers.

TANKARDS AND FLAGONS

When looking at a tankard or flagon with a view to deciding its place of origin there are several features which must be analysed. Because tankards and flagons were for so long the very essence of pewter (not forgetting dishes) it is vital for the collector to understand them and to get a feel for the nature of pieces made in different districts. The area which this chapter attempts to cover is enormous. Sometimes you will have to be content with the knowledge that a piece was made "somewhere in central Europe" without being able to pinpoint its town of origin.

The variety of basic body shapes and sizes is very great – a number of these are dealt with below. Apart from the overall shape of the body, characteristic German features include: a

Right A flagon of the *Rörken* type from north Germany, inscribed at the lip "Wer Kreutz und Leuthen nicht hat der lesch diesen Reimen ab" and engraved with symbols of the masons and carpenters guild; 18th century, 13¼in.

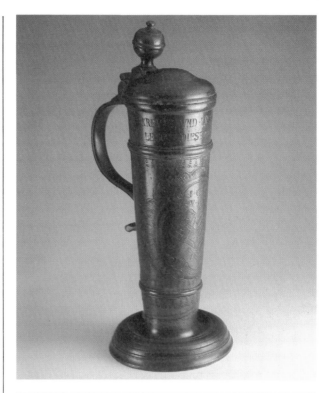

Flagons from, *left to right*, Cologne, 17th-18th century, 6½in; Austria-Hungary, 18th century, 9¾in; Austria, 17th century, 5½in.

flat-topped domed cover (few German drinking vessels lack a cover), the shape of the dome (curved, slanting or straight) varying from region to region; a ball thumbpiece (there are numerous designs of this type); a double-C erect thumbpiece; in Austria and Hungary, a mascaron thumbpiece or a plumed thumbpiece; marks inside the cover or at the top of the handle; in the north, a flat projecting base; in the south, a beak-like spout; in Austria, the handle terminal flush with the

Right A tankard, the body moulded into lobed panels, marked on the handle by Hans Jacob Seifertold of Hall, Württemberg; 17th century, 7¼in.

Left   Rörken from Lübeck, by Hinrich Helmcke; c. 1655, 8½in.

body, often with mascaron terminal. It must be remembered that whereas in France wine was the most popular drink throughout the country and in all social classes, in Germany a large amount of beer was consumed as well as wine.

The *Rörken* is a flagon which comes mainly from the north (e.g. Lübeck, Bremen, Rostock) although, as always, there is the occasional exception. Examples are always of fine quality and usually inscribed – many for guild use. The body is of slender V-shaped form, tapering inwards towards the moulded base; the cover may be single- or double-domed, and there is a variety of thumbpieces: ridged erect, plumed, ball or lion sejant. The marks are stamped at the top of the scroll handle. Rörken were made from the mid-17th to the mid-18th century.

In the northwest of Germany, near the border with the Netherlands (Ostfriesland) and near the Danish border, was made a plain cylindrical flagon with angular handle and erect thumbpiece. The body rests on a flat spreading foot (typical of the north, as previously mentioned); a simple knop centres the shallow domed cover which either has straight sides or a rounded edge curving inwards towards the lip.

A *Stitze* from Munich, c. 1730.

A *Stitze*, dated 1702, with the beak-like spout characteristic of the south. For a detail of the thumbpiece, see p. 36.

Further south, in Cologne, the native flagon has features in common with its Flemish and French neighbours. The slender neck is topped by a broad collar below the lip and the body flares into a bulbous central section above a cylindrical foot – sometimes this has a flat base similar to the flagons previously described. The cover is heart-shaped, usually with a small dome, and with an erect thumbpiece and a scroll handle.

In the southwest (in Ulm, Württemberg, and in Munich, for example) a shape is found which is very similar to that of the Swiss *Sugerli* – indeed hanging vessels of that type were also made in this part of Germany. These flagons have a bombé body and a scroll handle; the cover is shallow-domed with a ball finial. They were made with and without a spout.

Stitzen are found in Austria and southern Germany, similar to those made in Switzerland. The basic body shape (tapering cylindrical with a flat base) does not alter very much and all have a scroll handle. Austrian examples can often be distinguished by the handle ending flush with the body in a mascaron terminal. As has already been pointed out, this is a typical Austrian feature found on many designs of tankard and flagon. The covers vary considerably but nearly all have an erect thumbpiece.

Schnabelstitzen (spouted flagons) do not follow this rule, however. As well as having the erect thumbpiece, in Germany and Austria schnabelstitzen were also made with the ball thumbpiece, although this is never combined with a

Left A *Schnabelstitze* or spouted flagon, by Joseph Apeller of Innsbruck; 18th century, 7in.

Above A flagon from the southwest; Nuremberg, early 19th century; 4½in.

cover finial. The body of a stitze was sometimes moulded into swirling panels – or punched to resemble such curves. Late 18th- and 19th-century flagons often rest on feet of winged cherub masks – reviving a much earlier feature (see p. 206).

The spout of German flagons is of the triangular beak-like form and it appears on pieces of very varied proportions – from the short and squat to the tall and slender. Spouted flagons of various designs, not only stitzen, are found throughout Austria and southern Germany and up the Rhine to Cologne, where the influence of this tradition on Strasbourg pewterers is, of course, important.

Pear-shaped or baluster tankards come primarily from central Germany: Silesia, Saxony and Thuringia. The shape of the baluster varies according to the date of the piece – late 18th- and 19th-century examples are more slender than their predecessors. They nearly always have a ball thumbpiece and the cover is of flat-topped domed type; the body tucks into a spreading base.

Transylvanian pewterers retained an affinity in their work with the earlier Breslau (now Wroclaw) Silesian flagons. Its troubled history, with constant interference from eastern

Above An Austrian spouted measure, with beak-like spout; 18th century.

Right A German flagon attractively engraved with hunting scenes, mid-17th century, 12in.

Below An 18th-century tankard with the ovolo moulded foot popular particularly in Saxony and north-central Germany.

invaders and frequent change of rulers, affected Hungary's artistic development, but through the centuries Upper Hungary and Transylvania maintained a fine tradition of craftsmanship. In the late 17th century, Schassburg was an important centre for the making of flagons. The tall slender, cylindrical bodies had domed covers centred by a finial (often tiered). The body was often covered with engraving, either pictorial or abstract: hunting scenes were popular, also foliate ornament. Hungarian pewter continued to be decorated by engraving and relief work after these had ceased

Two guild tankards, one with a plain ball thumbpiece, probably from Eberswalde northeast of Berlin, dated 1723 (8¾ in), the other, with brass medallion in high relief and showing rococo features, from Salzburg, dated 1783 (9¼in). Both are engraved with the names of guild members and their towns of origin.

Below right Pewter mounts: on a Meissen tankard, c. 1735, 9in; on salt-glazed stoneware from Frechen, c. 1600, 9½in; on German faience, mid 18th century, 10in.

elsewhere. It was the custom for Hungarian pewterers to import pieces from Germany, decorate them and stamp them with their own mark. The use of stamped ornament at borders was popular too. This type of decoration is seen throughout southern Germany, particularly in Augsburg, on a wide range of items – not only flagons.

Tankards of cylindrical form were made in most parts of Germany throughout the 18th and first half of the 19th century. They were made in a multitude of capacities and sizes and bear a closer resemblance to tankards made by contemporary silversmiths than any of the others mentioned. The majority had a ball thumbpiece and the domed cover had no finial. The barrel of these tankards often had engraved armorials or inscriptions but the cover was also frequently inscribed. Marks were stamped inside the lid in the 18th century or, less frequently, on the handle back, a practice continued from the 17th century. The variations in style of these cylindrical tankards and flagons are infinite and it is, in a sense, ridiculous to try to class them together simply because there is a similarity of body shape.

MOUNTED ITEMS

The domed cover with ball thumbpiece was also popular as a mount for glass and pottery tankards. In the mid-18th century they often showed a touch of rococo influence, with fluting on the curve of the dome. Pewter had been a popular form of mount since the 16th century; its simplicity was a fitting contrast to the different glazes and textures. A wide range of Rhenish stoneware jugs and flagons, from potteries for example at Siegburg, Cologne and Kreussen, was made with metal mounts which bore little resemblance stylistically

Right A *Pechkrug*, its sides of wooden staves overlaid with pewter, from Lichtenhain/Thuringia; 18th century, 6in. *Far right* A flask from Kreussen with pewter mounts; 2nd half 17th century, 7½in.

Left A serpentine tankard with pewter mounts, the upper part of the body carved in triangular facets, by Frantz Pfister of Nuremberg, c. 1645–65, 7in.

to contemporary pewterware. Specialist pewter lid makers developed their own styles.

Whereas mounted pottery jugs were made elsewhere, notably in the Netherlands, mounted wooden tankards (*Pechkrug*) are native to Germany. They are usually of cylindrical or squat tapering form, with a shallow domed cover and ball thumbpiece (rarely, a lion thumbpiece). The body has vertical wooden staves inlaid with pewter, cast into the wood and then finished by being cut in designs of foliage, scrolls or animals (notably lions) and hunting scenes. Most of these tankards were made in Thuringia in the 18th century.

The dark green hue of serpentine was also considered a good foil for pewter mounts – not only in tankards but flasks also. The stone has a wonderfully rich texture and varying density of colour. Pieces were often cut in elaborate designs and then mounted very simply in pewter.

FLASKS

The screw-top flask (*Schraubflasche*) was made in southern Germany and Austria from the 17th to the 19th centuries. Its form is just like those made in neighbouring Switzerland – most are hexagonal or octagonal – a design which continued for three centuries, with differences only in decoration. By the late 18th and 19th centuries this shape and the simple cylindrical design were virtually the only types made, but in the 17th and early 18th centuries there had been great variety. The polygonal shapes of early Silesian flagons were adapted for flasks; the body was moulded into deep swirling curves or vertical flutes; another style was of flat rectangular form with pronounced "shoulders". These pieces were seldom left plain. Earlier flasks were covered with decoration, each facet differently designed with contrasting or complementary ornament. In the early 17th century the relief decoration was usually of figures, in the tradition of *Edelzinn*; this gave way to bold baroque foliage, both engraved and cast or chased in relief. By the 18th century engraving (particularly the use of wrigglework) had superseded relief-work. Nineteenth-century flasks are usually plain, or simply engraved with owner's initials. The handle of a flask is nearly always of the drop-ring type – either plain or cast with beading, moulding or grotesques.

In the late 18th and the 19th centuries spouts were sometimes added to flasks. The piece is then known as a *Schraubkanne*. The makers tried to vary these, either using a simple cylindrical design of spout or, with the advent of neo-classicism, branching out into curves and animal heads. The addition of a side handle further distorted the original proportions of the piece.

Left A tea caddy engraved at the borders and on the cover with scrolling foliage; 6in. *Right* A large strawberry dish, the border fluted into 12 panels; 10½in. Both c. 1740.

Above Ewer and basin unmarked but possibly by Klingling of Frankfurt, who made very similar pieces in the 18th century; ewer 7½in, basin 12½in.

Left An oval sugar box, mid -18th century, 6in.

ROCOCO

Up to the early 18th century the pewterer's repertoire had been restricted almost entirely to the making of tankards, flagons, plates, flasks and guild pieces. Domestic equipment had not yet played an important part in his work. All this was to change around 1730 when the Germans went wild over rococo. The most popular aspect of rococo in Germany was the use of curved moulding. Coffee pots, teapots, salt cellars, soup tureens, bowls, candlesticks and plates were enlivened in this manner; not even tankards escaped. Most of these pieces are in the style of contemporary work in silver and porcelain. Early pieces (1720–40) have "straight-fold" decoration, then the moulded folds begin to swirl round the body. Inevitably the quality of this domestic pewter is varied – a large quantity was produced, much of it inferior, for the mass market. This was the pewterers' final fling in the face of the growing popularity of pottery and porcelain. Many of these pieces are unmarked, some are stamped only with the quality mark. As we shall see (p. 130) much of the rococo pewter now found in Switzerland was most probably made in Germany and goods were undoubtedly exported to other countries as well.

LATE 18TH- AND EARLY 19TH-CENTURY DOMESTIC PEWTER

Rococo continued to be popular with pewterers for the rest of the 18th century. The next major influence was neo-classicism. The use of this style was quite widespread, even

Two coffee pots, mid 18th century (*left*) and 1st half 19th century (*right*).

though by the end of the century the industry was in decline. Coffee pots, milk jugs, soup tureens, candlesticks, for example, are quite readily available to the present-day collector. The plain clear-cut lines were occasionally enlivened by decorative borders and stiff leafage. This simplicity continued through the era known as "Biedermeier", with its more rounded, cosier forms. Engraving was limited to owner's initials and dates.

Not all domestic pewter conformed to these easily defined styles. In the late 18th and early 19th centuries food containers of simple designs were made throughout the country. In the northwest, pear-shaped tea and coffee urns and teapots were popular, which are often indistinguishable from those made in the Netherlands. Simple two-handled bowls resting on three feet and with covers were made in the north. These have much in common with Scandinavian pieces. Ewers and basins tended to be made in the prevailing styles of the time.

A wall salt, probably from Nuremberg; 1st half 19th century, 8in.

A circular tureen, with drop ring handles; early 19th century.

CANDLESTICKS AND LAMPS

Candlesticks, too, always reflect the changes in fashion. Until the late 17th century these were nearly always of pricket type. During the 18th century pricket candlesticks were usually made only for church use, although some of the smaller ones may have been for the home. In the late 17th and early 18th centuries these altar candlesticks usually had a triform base of baroque taste which supported a high baluster stem; the pricket or sconce rested in a circular drip-pan. The stem and base were often decorated with winged cherub masks, acanthus leafage, scrolls and other foliate ornament.

A design of candlestick which is now popular (hence the large number of reproductions) is the miner's stick (*Bergmannsleuchter*). A man dressed in 18th-century costume stands on a variously designed base. In one raised hand he holds a sconce. These were made in the 18th century in Saxony, Thuringia and Bohemia.

Another form of lighting was the oil lamp. Most of those seen today date from the late 18th and early 19th centuries. These usually have a slender cylindrical stem with carrying handle supported on a circular dished base. Most of the variations of style are in the oil container. The most common German form is an hemispherical bowl with the wick either protruding direct from the bowl or, in slightly more sophisticated examples which have a cover to the container, the wick extends from a curved tube protruding from the bowl. Others have vertical glass containers for the oil, some of which have the hours marked on the straps holding the glass (these were also made in France). Hanging wall lamps are another variety.

Left A pair of 18th-century pricket altar candlesticks with the usual baroque triform base, high baluster stem, drip-pan and ornament including foliage; 28in.

Right Two oil lamps, standing (11in) and hanging (7in); late 18th/early 19th century.

Below An oil lamp, c. 1800, 13¾in. In some examples the glass oil reservoir is held in pewter straps marked with the hours against which to read the oil level.

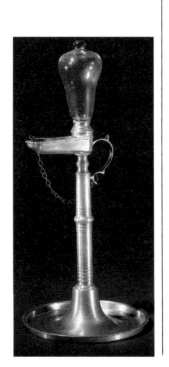

DISHES AND PLATES

German and Austrian plates differ slightly from those made in, for example, France and the Netherlands. The multiple-reeding which was popular in England around 1700 did not find favour here. Nor did the Germans engrave the broad rims of their dishes in the 17th century with armorials, as did the French, Swiss and English. They did, however, engrave initials and sometimes the entire name of the owner, particularly in the 18th and early 19th centuries. Plates at this time tend to have fairly narrow, plain borders, sometimes with a single band of reeding. And, of course, the rococo style was popular in the second half of the 18th century. Bowls (with no rims) were also made in large quantities. From the mid-18th century onwards many plates and dishes were engraved all over in a variety of styles and techniques – simple line engraving, wrigglework and punched motifs. Designs differ greatly – vases of flowers, animals, armorials (the arms of Saxony are frequently seen) or scenes from everyday life.

Some of these plates were made or were adapted for religious use and are engraved in Hebrew script. The most usual are engraved on the rim with the order of the Passover Eve Service. Some, though, are simply engraved with Hebraic initials on the rim or on the underside of the plate. Others are covered with engraving all round the border and in the well.

The combination of line and wrigglework engraving was

particularly popular in Hungary. Transylvanian pewterers covered the whole surface of a dish with a mass of entwined ornament. In the 17th century hexagonal plates were a popular design.

When a plate is elaborately engraved in the well it is unlikely that it was used a great deal – it would have been displayed on a dresser or sideboard. This must apply, also, to

Left A fine 16th-century plate with central boss; 8in. The border is stamped with an unidentified housemark, and with touchmarks probably of Sebastian Tenter of Leipzig, made a master in 1565.

Below A plain bowl and a wavy-edged plate, both late 18th or early 19th century; 8¾in.

Right A plate depicting Adam and Eve, in which line and wrigglework engraving are used; dated 1687, 16in.

scale plates. These are flat discs of pewter originally intended for the serving of cakes, cheeses and the like. Their surface was ideally suited for displaying the engraver's art and he lavished a great deal of attention of them. Some (particularly late 16th- and early 17th-century examples) have scenes copied from contemporary prints. Later in the 17th century heraldry was used and throughout the 17th and early 18th centuries genre scenes and formal motifs were portrayed. Many were pierced (some to such an extent as to be totally impractical) and all had a pierced hole at the border so that the plate could be hung on the wall.

SWITZERLAND

The linguistic and cultural divisions of Switzerland are reflected in its pewter. Stylistic features cross the borders with France, Germany and Austria. This is more apparent in flagons and measures than in dishes and plates, or the pewter made in the rococo style. The flagons typify the Swiss talent for harmonizing diverse elements. The success of this blending, this pulling together of component styles, partly explains the enormous popularity and demand for Swiss pewter among collectors today. Wine cans and stitzen similar to those from the northeastern cantons are found in southern Germany and Austria, whilst in Valais and Vaud measures have features in common with the French and Italian.

A commemorative plate from St Gallen, the centre with three figures symbolizing the revolt of three forest cantons against the Hapsburgs, the border shaped into 13 sections bearing the arms of the Swiss cantons; 16th century, 8½in.

FRANCE

NEUCHÂ
(NEUNBE
Neuc

VAUD

Lausanne

L Geneva

GENEVA Geneva
(GENF)

SAVOY

PIEDM

| 0 | | 40km |
| 0 | | 30mi |

Switzerland is a federation formed by cantons drawn together from parts of what were the imperial kingdoms of Germany, Italy and Burgundy. People from these lands came together solely for the purpose of defence – initially against the Hapsburgs. The popular stories of Hapsburg oppression (including the legend of William Tell) are based on the division of loyalties between Emperor Frederick II and the Hapsburgs before and after the former's excommunication by Innocent IV in 1245. The death of Rudolph of Hapsburg (who had been elected German king in 1273) paved the way for the league formed by men from the valleys of Uri, Schwyz and Unterwalden in 1291. A plate made in St Gallen, an example of which is in the Victoria and Albert Museum, commemorates the formation of the league and the taking of the oath of Ruetli in 1308. Cast in relief, the central boss depicts three men, symbolizing the league's originators, and the 13 sections of the border bear the arms of the increased number of cantons in the league at the time of the plate's manufacture in the 16th century. This number remained unaltered until 1798, despite frequent territorial changes, the latest major one being the annexation of Geneva and Vaud in the early 16th century. The German cantons, however, were always dominant.

Divided by religion at this time, as a consequence of the

The chief pewter-making towns and the cantons of Switzerland.

Reformation, the 13 cantons were re-united in their agreement to defend their frontiers during the Thirty Years War, in spite of the fact that Swiss mercenaries fought on both sides. By the Treaty of Westphalia in 1648 Emperor Ferdinand III renounced all former Hapsburg claims for Swiss territory. The political and religious dissensions of the 17th and 18th centuries led to power developing in various sectors of the communities – the aristocracy, the trade guilds, the military. There were several rebellious uprisings. Switzerland was invaded by the French in 1798: the Confederation was dissolved and a Helvetian Republic established. Napoleon reconstituted the confederation with 19 cantons in 1803. In 1815 the Congress of Vienna added Geneva, Valais and Neuchâtel and all 22 cantons (the present number: see map) signed the Pact of Confederation. However, religious and social unrest continued, until the new federal state was formed in 1848. But, for over 550 years, between 1291 and 1848, each canton functioned separately.

Switzerland's geographical position and scenic beauty made her a natural centre for travellers, and there was continual movement of people and ideas. The 17th and 18th centuries were a period of great intellectual and artistic development. Although Swiss pewterers were familiar with fashions throughout Europe and made pieces in the current styles, they never lost sight of their local traditions and the cantons developed, and largely preserved, their distinctive styles of decoration and variants in form. They produced works of the finest quality, as did Swiss goldsmiths and enamellers.

FLAGONS AND MEASURES

Flagons and measures have no stylistic counterparts in pieces made by contemporary goldsmiths, and they most strongly reflect regional differences. By the late 17th century the style of each type of flagon had evolved and remained almost the same until the mid-19th century. But within what might appear at first sight to be a rather limited repertoire, there is immense variety of decorative detail. And if it were possible to gather together a large number of any one type of flagon, one could see more easily the range of shapes achieved within the confines of traditional style.

The heart-shaped cover is the principal feature common to the flagons from the central, south and west cantons – those with French and Italian connections. In Valais (or Wallis) and Vaud was made the powerful *Bauchkanne,* which comes in a range of sizes. It has a bulbous body (*bauch* means "bellied"), and an incurved neck topped by a short collar and heart-shaped cover. One feature unique to Valais is the double ram's head thumbpiece found on larger specimens. Sometimes a third head is added as a finial, or to ring

SWITZERLAND

A *Kelchkanne* by André Utin of Vevey, the maker of the flagon on p. 120.

the changes, a ram's head finial might be seen with a twin-acorn or pomegranate thumbpiece; or these thumbpieces with a dolphin finial. Differences are also found in the shape and length of the wedge across the cover from the thumb-piece.

The bauchkanne illustrated is by André Utin of Vevey. The same pewterer made *Stegkannen* and also the *Kelchkanne* illustrated, which shows characteristics of many French pichets, as do most of the measures made round Lake Geneva. Kelchkannen have the heart-shaped cover and short collar above a narrow neck in common with the bauch-kannen, but the broad body below is shouldered and tapers only slightly inwards to the rim foot. Thumbpieces are twin-acorn, pomegranate or occasionally erect.

The upper body of both the kelchkannen and bauch-kannen is repeated in the much rarer *Bügelkanne*, but this time they sit on a flared faceted body and the piece has a swinging stirrup-like carrying handle or chain handle as an extra, similar to that found on some of the larger examples of its fellow Valais flagons, the bauchkannen. The heavy chain is a typical feature on Swiss flagons, whereas the stirrup handles are also seen in France.

The spouted flagon or *Stegkanne*, most commonly made in Berne but also made in Aargau, Fribourg and Vaud, would seem to derive its form, along with the celebrated "Jan Steen" flagons of Holland, from some common ancestry such as the earlier town or council flagons (illustrated p. 25) which in turn may be based on the Gothic dinanderie flagons and bronze lavers of the 13th to 15th centuries. The steg-kanne's origins in Switzerland can be seen in those 16th- and 17th-century flagons of which there are examples in the superb and comprehensive collection in the Schweizerisches Landesmuseum at Zurich. The bulbous body curves into a slender neck and expands slightly at the collar. The long spout is always faceted and connected to the collar, or just below, by a variously decorated supporting bar. This bar does not appear on the Dutch "Jan Steen" type, nor does the finial. The domed cover is usually surmounted by an acorn finial but Bernese stegkannen sometimes have a "blackamoor" or negro's head, similar to those on Dutch

A *Bügelkanne* (*left*) with stirrup carrying-handle and (*right*) a *Prismenkanne* with lidded spout, and screw-top lid and carrying-ring.

123

tobacco boxes. By the 17th century the simple scroll handle had developed a pronounced kink, which allowed room for a man's wrist if he held the flagon by its neck. Stegkannen were made of a fairly uniform size about 13in high. (A Bernese stegkanne is shown in the frontispiece of this book.) Fribourg retained the less pronounced belly and straight foot (this type is also found occasionally in Germany).

The body outline and handle of the stegkanne are very similar in the *Kurbiskanne* but this has no spout and the domed cover is replaced by the heart-shaped lid. The kurbiskanne might seem to share many features with the bauchkanne of Valais, but the proportions are quite different, the bauchkanne being of more massive outline. Stegkannen and kurbiskannen are usually marked on the handle, sometimes

A flagon *(Stitze)* by Bernhard Wick of Basle; 1st half 18th century, 11½in.

A spouted flagon (*Schnabel-stitze*) with acorn finial and plumed thumbpiece, by Samuel Bodmer of Berne; c. 1750, 8¼ in.

also on the lid, and stegkannen can also be found with marks on the hinged flap at the tip of the spout.

From the central area, crossing to the northern and eastern part of the country – and to German and Austrian influence – the type of flagon changes to the *Stitze*. Their proportions vary considerably: some are short and dumpy, others tall and slender. Of tapering cylindrical form, these flagons have bold scrolling handles which usually terminate in small ridged mouldings, unlike those we have already examined which end flush with the body or with only a tiny curl. There are two principal types, those with spouts and those without. The latter have flat covers, sometimes with a slight peak in the centre – a token finial looking as though it lacks the strength to break through and form the real thing. But other spoutless stitzes do have true finials. When the flagon has a spout it is known as a schnabelstitze. The spout (the like of which occurs also in Germany and Austria) is short and beak-like; when viewed sideways-on it is of moulded triangular form; it is capped by an extension of the

cover. By way of variation this spout sometimes sports a bearded human mask; it is then termed *Bartmannstitze*. Thumbpieces are usually erect or plumed.

Two flagons which are made in the northern cantons should be mentioned briefly. The *Rundele* had the same extremities – beak-like spout, thumbpiece and scroll handle – as the stitze, but the body is baluster-shaped, not tapering. The other is the *Kugelkrug*, which is a rare type made around 1700.

WINE CANS AND TANKARDS

Stitzen comparable to the schnabelstitzen were made in Germany and so too were spouted wine cans, which were carried by means of a leather strap slung through the ring holder, either over a man's shoulder or attached to a mule. There are two main designs of wine can which overlap geographically and which span regional boundaries. They are called *Glockenkanne* and *Prismenkanne*. The former is bell-shaped the latter hexagonal.

To take the glockenkanne first, the circular body frequently has a shield applied – often at a slight angle – on which are engraved the initials or armorial bearings of the owner. It is encircled by varying bands of reeding and sometimes has additional engraving in the form of foliage around the spout. The spout is faceted and topped either by a hinged flap or a screw-on cap. The spool-shaped cover is either bayonet or screw-fitting and rises to a bold ring carrying handle. The hexagonal prismenkanne is very similar in most respects except the body shape. Coats-of-arms are often engraved direct onto the body below the spout.

Above, left to right A flagon of the *Rundele* type, with baluster body, the spout similar to those of some stitzen. *Centre* A conical measure from Fribourg; 2nd half 18th century, 11in. *Right* A *Kugelkrug*, this one from Basle with the body and cover chased with lobing; early 18th century, 6in.

Below right A tankard (*Humpen*) by Johannes Weber of Zurich, decorated overall with wrigglework foliage and interlaced motifs; mid-18th century, 8½in.

Below An engraved flask; late 18th century, 8¼in.

Both cans have derivatives in the *Glockenflasche* and *Prismenflasche*. These bottles or flasks (more likely to have contained broth than wine) have no spout and the screw-on covers sometimes have hinged rather than fixed carrying handles. All four types are usually marked on the covers; the wine cans also on their spout caps. There is remarkably little stylistic difference between the 17th and 19th centuries.

Last among the drinking or serving vessels, we come to tankards – *Humpen*. These were principally made in Zurich, although they are also found elsewhere in the northern cantons. Based very much on a German 17th-century silver model, the cylindrical body is usually enlivened with engraving. As well as erect or plumed thumbpieces, we also find ones with a shell-like fluted design. The scroll handle has a ridged terminal. They are usually 8–9in high.

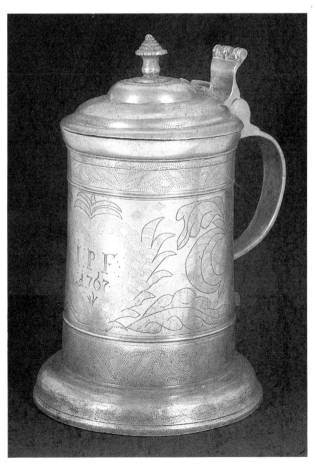

PLATES AND DISHES

Swiss plates are distinguished by a clarity of line which is rarely lost. The Swiss pewterer's sense of balance and proportion seldom left him. The making of flatware was less specialized than in some countries and makers of flagons also produced dishes; for example Abraham Ganting of Bern, Jean Charton of Geneva and members of the Bossard family of Zurich.

Throughout the 17th century dishes were broad-rimmed, with or without a raised boss in the centre. Unlike, for example, plates in England, this boss is seen as late as the early 18th century. Plain or moulded borders were made concurrently and regional differences are not as marked as those in hollow-ware. In the second half of the 17th century engraved armorials became an important feature, surrounded by foliate mantling or within simple crossed plumes. These were usually placed on the rim.

The entire plate was sometimes engraved with foliage – this was also a feature of the 18th century. These plates were most probably made for display; it is unlikely that they were used to serve food. Few plates which survive today bear traces of knife-cuts and the engraving on most is remarkably crisp. From the mid-18th century onwards a variety of scenes were engraved on plates, some having

Left A large example of the bell-shaped *Glockenkanne*, measuring 15¾in; a more usual size is 9–10in; 2nd half 18th century.

Above right A *Schnabelstitze* with pomegranate finial, by Emmanuel Streckeysen, Basle, c. 1780, 12in.

Left A single-reeded plate with relatively wide border, by Leonard Bourrelier; c. 1700, 8¾ in.

Right A cistern by Hans Luc(z)i de Cadenat(h) of Graubunden, Chur (1684–1720).

allegorical or religious significance, others depicting people in a rural or urban setting. Following the fashion prevailing in other countries, borders narrowed in the 18th century but were seldom plain – nearly always enlivened by reeded rims. This narrower border was also seen on deep bowls and other serving vessels, sometimes with drop-ring handles.

ROCOCO WARE
From about 1730 the rococo style played an important part in domestic pewterware. While many of the flagons and dishes which we have already discussed were being made, a whole range of domestic utensils was produced in this fashion, including plates, dishes, coffee pots, teapots, salt cellars, cruets, tureens, boxes and candlesticks. Much of it is unmarked, so it is difficult to be sure about where it was made (most of these are usually listed as "?Swiss"). A certain amount was made in Zurich and Zug, but a large proportion of rococo pewter found in Switzerland was most probably imported from Germany.

CAUDLE CUPS, CISTERNS AND SUGERLI
Although it is impossible to give a comprehensive survey of items made, three more characteristically Swiss objects must be mentioned.

The majority of *Sugerli* extant date from the 18th century and come from the northern cantons. The vessel hung

Left A *Sugerli*, probably
Swiss; mid-18th century,
7½in to finial.

Right A porringer (11in) and a
box with screw on cover
stamped with the sacred
monogram.

from a wall bracket and when tilted the water poured straight into the mouth of the drinker. The body is bombé, sometimes waisted below the swollen shoulder and with a moulded foot. The cover is hinged below the swing handle. This handle, usually made of iron, nearly always rises from human masks, whereas the spout emanates from a variety of grotesque or animal heads.

The wall cistern is also a water container, but for washing rather than drinking. Some are still found accompanied by their original pewter basin and frequently they were actually fitted into a sideboard surrounded by an alcove acting as a "splashback". A particularly appealing form of cistern is the dolphin, suspended head down, its tail curling upwards, and with the tap issuing from its mouth. Another variety is of pomegranate shape, another an acorn; these two are sometimes topped by a seated cherub or the familiar dolphin. These aquatic monsters were also popular decoration on the casket cisterns, whose diverse forms included rectangular, circular and cinquefoil designs, usually with a domed detachable lid. The body sometimes incorporated a recessed shelf, possibly reflecting the shape of the sideboard into which it was built.

Swiss écuelles and caudle cups and their covers again reflect the outside influences of France, Germany and the Low Countries. Unlike the majority of Swiss flagons, the

Porringer and cover of the 18th century; 8½in. The cover also served as a plate or stand, hence the three finials-cum-feet.

designs have close parallels in contemporary silver. The écuelle or *Ohrenschüssel* is a reflection of the French écuelle and it comes from the border lands. Further north, for example in Basel and Zurich, the body of the *Wochne-rinnenschüssel* (bowls traditionally given to women in labour) deepens and becomes more bulbous but still retains the flat pierced handles. When the cover has three finials (or feet) it can be placed upside down and used as a plate. However, in these towns another type was made, with pomegranate feet from the northern tradition and openwork handles of the type seen on Dutch brandy bowls, incorporating scrolls and caryatids.

ENGRAVING

From the late 17th century onwards the most popular form of decoration on Swiss pewter is engraving. Display pewter (*Edelzinn*) was never as popular here as in Germany. Reeding is used to decorate the bodies of flagons and tankards or the borders of dishes. And, of course, a variety of combinations of thumbpieces and finials are seen. Wriggle-work engraving was very popular and was used to depict flowers, foliage and scrolling ornament in a multitude of designs. When engraving owners' initials, names or a

An inkstand, by F. Cane or Canis of Appenzell; c. 1800, 5in. The well lid is missing.

commemorative inscription, the Swiss engraver of the 18th century (in common with many continental counterparts) frequently used two or three lines rather than just one for the vertical stroke of a letter (see illustration p. 34).

SOME FAMOUS PEWTERERS

Family tradition was strong amongst Swiss pewterers; generation followed generation in the same trade. In Zug, for example, members of the Keiser family made pewter for over two centuries. Other families whose works are among those most frequently seen today are the Bossard and Zimmerman families from Zurich, the Bauer family from Chur, members of the Charton family of Geneva. In Berne in the 18th century, Samuel Bodmer was a prolific maker of flagons as were Abraham and Jacob Ganting. In the same century Giovanni Tomas Tonietti and Vincent Variolly were working in Martigny and in the same canton (Valais) in the 19th century we find Giovanni del Barba. Close by in Vaud, André Utin of Vevey, who has already been mentioned, made in the 18th century a wide variety of plates, bauch-kannen, kelchkannen and stegkannen. Caspar Enderlein, who worked in Germany (see p. 94), was born in Switzerland.

ITALY

As far as is known, the making of pewter in Italy was almost entirely restricted to the north, the principal region being Piedmont. The paucity of Italian domestic pewter of all periods is curious and there is no very good explanation for it other than the continual process of melting down. Pewterers are known to have emigrated to Germany in fairly large numbers, apparently leaving few colleagues in Italy other than travelling workers.

Plates are amongst the most numerous of the pieces which have survived. In the 16th and 17th centuries plates were chased with bold lobing and engraved with entwined strapwork and leafage. During the 18th century the balance of these two decorative features was reversed, engraving becoming dominant and relief work restricted to fairly narrow borders. The style of engraving is distinctive, being slightly naive, but boldy executed. One of the most frequently encountered designs on ornamented dishes of the 18th century is relief-cast fruit or floral rims. Petal lobing is also found on dishes.

Ecclesiastical pewter must also have been made quite extensively; the items which can most easily be found today include holy water buckets and sanctuary lamps.

Piedmontese pewterers apparently made measures of very similar form to those of their neighbours in Valais, notably the bauchkanne.

Today pewter is still made in the north in centres such as Brescia, Milan and Cremona and, to a lesser extent, in

A north Italian ewer and basin; mid-17th century, 8¼in high and 14in wide.

A plate engraved with a grotesque mask within a raised border of various fruits; probably Venetian or Piedmontese, 18th or 19th century; 11¼in.

A late 18th or early 19th-century plate engraved with an historical subject, Pasquale Cicogna, Doge of Venice, 1565–95; 9¼in.

Left Two flagons, the left one particularly showing the form typical in the 17th and 18th centuries; 9½in.

Right Typical candlesticks with the Iberian bulbous base and short stem; 18th or 19th century, 5¼ and 6¾in.

central Italy. Modern pewterers make many pieces reproducing the style of earlier fashions.

Tin was mined early in the Iberian peninsula, but the quality of the metal used for a range of objects is generally very low. The items from Spain and Portugal which are most commonly seen today are ewers and basins, candlesticks and flagons. Many of the candlesticks come from churches and of course other items of ecclesiastical pewter, such as chalices, chrismatories, sanctuary lamps and holy water stoups, are known, just as the range of domestic pewter was fairly extensive.

Flagons of the 17th and 18th centuries have great affinity with Low Countries measures and earlier Hanseatic pieces. The body has a cylindrical neck which broadens to a rather low-slung bulge above a spreading foot. The cover is domed, almost hemispherical, and usually has a thumbpiece that is of plain erect form. The handle is a scrolling strap.

Ewers and basins date mainly from the 18th century. The basins are oval, with plain or wavy-edged borders, usually with a moulded rim. These basins sometimes have a crescent cut out of the border so that it can be tucked under a man's chin for shaving. The accompanying ewer is helmet-shaped, the lower part of the body being bulbous and encircled by moulded bands, and it rests on a stepped domed base. The handle is either caryatid or scrolling.

The average height of Iberian candlesticks is between 5½in and 7½in. The short stem rises from a bulbous base on a rim foot and has an acorn-shaped sconce.

LOW COUNTRIES

In Roman times, pewterers in the Low Countries, as in the rest of Europe, were chiefly dependent on tin from Cornwall. Gradually other mines were worked and in the early 16th century the Dutch East Indies began to produce an ever-increasing quantity of ore, brought home by the Dutch East India Company. Undoubtedly families of pewterers worked together, maintaining their skills from one generation to another. The work of some Low Countries pewterers is found today more frequently than others, but partly because records are less complete than elsewhere and partly because research is still being done into such records as there are, we know the names and histories of comparatively few of the hundreds of pewterers who worked in the region.

Dutch and Flemish pewter has a close affinity to that of England and Scotland. Certain alloys in both regions are susceptible to tin pest because of the damp climates. Early Low Countries pewter has a compactness and chunkiness of form which gives it great character. It reflects the life-style of its peoples, who expected to use wares of good quality but who had no court life to which they could aspire, either on the local level of the numerous German principalities or such as the cultural centre of the court of Louis xiv. There is very little decoration on pewter from the Low Countries – emphasis was placed on form and colour. Relief decoration, such as that found in Germany and France, is virtually unknown, except on the occasional early handle, and engraving is generally limited to inscriptions and armorials.

There was great movement of population, as boundaries changed and as the prosperity of regions altered. The sacking of Antwerp in 1585, for example, brought to an end the supremacy which that city had enjoyed throughout the Middle Ages. Hundreds of people, including pewterers, moved north to Amsterdam, which rapidly developed. Later, Rotterdam became another major port. These cities influenced the lives of people in the surrounding lands, and their craftsmen sent work for sale in the country which was imitated by local pewterers.

Because of the joint heritage of the Low Countries (what we know today as The Netherlands, Belgium and Luxembourg), it is frequently impossible to know with certainty whether a piece of pewter is Dutch or Flemish. By the Middle Ages the area consisted of several small principalities and bishoprics which had feudal relationships with the Holy Roman Empire and France. In the 13th century the prosperity and civic dignity of the Low Countries, based principally on the wool trade, were almost unrivalled. The reclamation of marshland and the building of dykes produced good agricultural land, cloth became a major industry, especially in the south, and the many ports, linked to the rest

Pewter-making towns in the Low Countries, showing the frontiers of today and after the Treaty of Westphalia in 1648. Flanders and East Friesland are two of the regions where pewter traditions were stronger than the constraints of impermanent frontiers.

of the continent by the Rhine, the Meuse and the Scheldt, were centres of shipping and trade. Evidence of the importance of these ports is to be found in the "Hanseatic" pewter (see Introduction, pp. 16–18) made along the Baltic and North Sea coast in the 14th–16th centuries, which

GRONINGEN
•Leeuwarden   •Groningen
FRIESLAND

DRENTHE

Enkhuizen•
Hoorn•
HOLLAND   •Zwolle
Haarlem•   OVERYSSEL
Amsterdam•   •Deventer

NORTH SEA

UTRECHT
•Leiden
The Hague•   •Utrecht   GELDERLAND
•Delft   •Arnhem
Rotterdam•   •Schoonhoven
Waal   Nijmegen•

ZEELAND   •Breda
Middelburg•

•Antwerp

•Bruges
Dunquerque•   Ghent•   Scheldt
Calais   FLANDERS   LIEGE
BRABANT   Maastricht•
Leie   •Brussels

Lille•   Liège•
ARTOIS   HAINAUT
Namur•   Meuse
•Douai
•Arras

•Cambrai

boundary of the Netherlands
in the 17th century
present-day borders of Holland,
Belgium, Luxemburg, Germany and France

LUXEMBURG

Luxemburg•

0   60mi
0   80km

Above A beaker lightly
engraved with a portrait of
William of Orange (William III
of England) on horseback;
c. 1690, 6¾ in.

The genre paintings of Jan
Steen (1625–79) illustrate the
importance of pewter ware in
the tavern and middle-class
home. A pewter mounted
stoneware pitcher, a broad-
rimmed charger, a Dutch
round-bowled spoon, and (the
wine or beer being tried out
by a young child) a "Jan
Steen" spouted flagon feature
in this painting, *The Merry
Party* (1668).

includes the earliest dated flagon known from the Low Countries (1331).

Throughout the 13th and 14th centuries the Burgundians increased their influence and the French court acquired works of art from the Low Countries, but with the marriage of Mary of Burgundy to Maximilian in 1477, the Hapsburgs became established in the Low Countries. During the early 16th century the Low Countries were in turmoil because of the Reformation. Calvinism became the driving force against Catholic Spain. William "the Silent", Prince of Orange, became the leader of this resistance, but he was also a member of a club, the "Illustrious Brotherhood of Our Lady", founded to foster good relations between the religions. A fine group of flagons survives from this club (including one bearing William's coat-of-arms).

Although William hoped for a United Netherlands, the seven northern Protestant provinces joined together in 1579 as the United Provinces, and the south (roughly modern Belgium and Luxembourg) confirmed its loyalty to the Spanish king and the catholic religion. It was at this time that the northerners came to be called Hollanders or Netherlanders (or Dutch by the English) and the people of the south Flemings.

Despite internal dissension (both religious and social), the United Provinces became one of the most prestigious nations, whilst involved in almost continuous wars. The most powerful and economically strong of the United Provinces was Holland; Amsterdam was one of the principal financial centres in Europe and Dutch shipping carried three-quarters of the world's produce. In 1596 an attempt to extend this shipping had ended in disaster, when the expedition foundered at the island of Novaya Zemlya. It left behind pewter candlesticks, flagons and standing salts which give us an insight into late 16th century domestic pewter, of which little else survives. The group (which is now in the Rijksmuseum, Amsterdam) is often named after the captain of the expedition, Heemskerk.

In 1689 William III of Orange accepted the crown of England with his wife Mary, daughter of the deposed King James II. Thus a long tradition of close relations with England, which had only occasionally been broken by war (notably in the previous thirty years), culminated in the joint reign of William III and Mary II. The event is commemorated in pewter in both countries, an example of which is the beaker illustrated. While the Dutch favoured beakers as the most suitable commemorative item, the English made plates and tankards. Many Dutch beakers were exported to England.

The 17th century was an era of tremendous economic expansion and cultural splendour. In this golden age, the influence of Dutch and Flemish artists and craftsmen such as Rembrandt, Rubens, Franz Hals and members of the van Vianen family of goldsmiths, spread throughout Europe. The wealthy merchant classes demanded goods of fine quality for use in their homes. No longer were their orders restricted to pieces for guild, corporation and church use. Initially this most probably benefitted goldsmiths more than pewterers, whose metal was not suitable for the finely chased pieces of the "auricular" style or the superb engraving for which the Netherlands also gained international renown in the early 17th century. The middle to late 17th century was the time of the tulip craze, when vast amounts of money were spent on the purchase and cultivation of rare bulbs. And so this flower is seen on those few pieces of pewter which were decorated, for example Friesian brandy bowls, and this decorative feature continued into the next century.

After the tremendous burst of energy of the previous hundred years the 18th century was a period of consolidation and relative decline. However, the country remained autonomous and strongly independent. The home-loving nature of the Dutch and Flemish, so noticeable in 17th-century painting, is evident in the domestic wares which have survived from the 18th century.

We can see how pewter was used – and abused – through contemporary painting and in particular Dutch and Flemish painting of the 16th and 17th centuries. Interior scenes of domestic and tavern life show flagons being filled from wine butts and in turn being emptied into mugs, glasses and smaller drinking flagons, which were left casually on the floor or table. The sober nature of the pewter is at variance with the convivial atmosphere of the inns. The popular, if rather moralistic, subject of drunkenness (particularly in women) was frequently depicted by seated figures slouched over a table bearing a pewter flagon. In the home when not in use flagons were hung on the wall or placed on shelves (often upside down to dry, with the lids hanging over the edge) whilst dishes lined the walls and chimneybreast. The still-life painter skillfully selected contrasting objects and it is left to the eye of the beholder to decide which item steals the show – the plainness and solidity of the pewter beside the highly decorated contemporary silver; the dark sheen of the base metal next to piles of fruit and glass.

FLAGONS

The general form of pewter drinking vessel or decanter from the Low Countries is bulbous or pear-shaped with a lid. Made in a wide range of sizes, they are usually termed flagons – a few tankards were made (usually of slightly concave form) but they found little favour here compared with Germany and England. Similarly measures are found in relatively small quantities and these take much the same

145

form as flagons but have no lid. The lip of measures is often covered by capacity seals, stamped by the inspector when checking them. Early flagons were, as a general rule, neat and dumpy. This stoutness of form gives way in the 16th century and the Golden Age of the 17th to greater elegance and confidence, features which are lost in the general malaise of the 18th century when flagons degenerated into a style which is weak by comparison. The primary use of these vessels would have been for serving liquid into stoneware, wood and pewter beakers, but they were also used to drink from. By the 18th century the increased use of glass and the development of porcelain and earthenware (Delftware) resulted in pewter flagons being used only for dispensing drink. As the small drinking flagons went completely out of use the size of flagons was limited to the larger quantities. (It must not be forgotten that many stoneware flagons and tankards were given pewter lids.)

A concave-sided tankard with twin ball thumbpiece; Rotterdam, 1600.

As elsewhere, it is the detail which gives us a clue to date. Early thumbpieces were of the twin-ball and hammer types and from 1400 to 1600 these, together with twin-acorn (also found in France, the Channel Islands and Switzerland), are most common. They rest at the end of a heavy wedge linking hinge and cover. In the 17th century the "erect" thumbpiece came into fashion and the cover wedge virtually disappeared. Throughout this time, the hinge would be of either single or double type, although the former tends to be earlier. The erect thumbpiece continued through the 18th century although it lost favour to the less substantial shell design. Handles in the Middle Ages were of semi-circular form (with a curved face on the inside) but this gave way to a simple strap until in the 18th century we see also a scrolling cylindrical form.

One of the most prolific 17th-century genre painters was Jan Steen, whose works nearly always contain a piece of pewter. His name has been given to a type of spouted flagon which was in existence long before his time. One of the earliest examples of this beautifully balanced flagon can be seen in the famous painting by Cornelis Anthonisz in the Rijksmuseum of *A Shooting Club Dinner* (1533), but the style can be seen even earlier in a 14th-century flagon now in the Historisches Museum in Basle (compare the Swiss stegkanne shown in the frontispiece).

Above A "Jan Steen" spouted flagon, a large dish to carry the meat, and a "Rembrandtkan" are among the pewter table ware in this 1533 group portrait, *A Shooting Club Dinner*, by Cornelis Anthonisz (c. 1499–1557), now in the Amsterdam Historical Museum.

Right A "Jan Steen" flagon made in the 17th century, 10¼in, and two examples of "Lambskan" with maker's mark wk inside the lid; 18th century, 5in.

"Jan Steen" flagons were used for decanting drink, whereas another form of spouted flagon was used for drinking – or rather sucking. Of much squatter form, these "lamb's flagons" (or "sucking flagons") have narrow cylindrical spouts protruding from either the neck or the base. The handles are set at right-angles to or opposite the spout. In spite of their name, it is much more likely that they were used to feed invalids or children than lambs.

At the beginning of the 17th century a style of flagon was made which was unusual because it is almost identical to silver flagons made in England and is probably derived from German guild flagons. The high domed foot of this flagon is also seen on many of the guild and council flagons which were made at this time.

The Dutch were fond of nicknames, both for their rulers and for their possessions. The type of flagon called "Rembrandtkan" has no connection with the painter and like other nicknames was probably a 19th-century invention. Distinguished by a wide cylindrical band at the neck, the body outline is also baluster or pear-shaped – rather similar to that of the Jan Steen. A Rembrandtkan has a shallow domed cover, often with a circular disc in the centre on which is sometimes engraved the owner's name or initials.

A group of flagons ("Rembrandtkan") of the 17th and 18th centuries; 4–11in.

Above A pear-shaped flagon from Maastricht with spout and shell thumbpiece; 18th century, 13½in.

Right A pear-shaped spouted flagon, with double-scroll handle and shell thumbpiece. This fairly common form is found with a range of variations in handle and thumbpiece, in the late 18th and early 19th centuries. The average size is 8–10in.

The marks are also frequently stamped on the lid, unlike later flagons which are marked on the underside of the base or lid. (It was not the custom to stamp marks on the handle as in, for example, Germany and Switzerland.) Most existing examples of Rembrandtkan are late 16th- and 17th- century (they were made until about 1730–40) but they were more popular throughout the late 16th and 17th centuries. Their size varied considerably. Many were used in guilds, and these are usually of particularly fine quality and good proportions. Some are covered with inscriptions and, unlike those for domestic use, have tiered finials, which add a touch of grandeur – no doubt considered suitable by the worthy burghers who drank from them. They were proud of their pewter, which must have played an important part in the life of the guild or club to which they belonged or, in the case of town or council flagons, their municipal life. In the many group portraits which were painted, we see up to ten or fifteen men round a table holding their drinking flagons. The table is either littered with the remains of a banquet (served on pewter) or is covered by a carpet on which rests the flagon from which they have filled their individual vessels.

A style of flagon developed towards the end of the 17th

149

LOW COUNTRIES

Left A flagon, most probably from a church, late 17th or early 18th century, 12in, and a pear-shaped flagon, 18th century, 10in.

Above Metric measures, Flemish or from northeast France, both 19th century. They are of litre and demi-litre capacity, and the inspectors' marks stamped on the smaller one are in both Roman and Greek alphabets; 8½ and 7in.

century which was to be made throughout the 18th and 19th centuries with only slight variations. These flagons are one of the types of item most readily available to present-day collectors. The shape most probably derived from the Rembrandtkan; the general outline is pear-shaped with a shallow domed cover and short rim base. They vary in size between approximately 8in and 10in high. At the beginning of the 18th century the handle was a simple strap and the thumbpiece was erect. The erect thumbpiece continued to be used throughout the century but with the advent of the shell form, the more usual combination seen is that flagons with a spout have a shell thumbpiece and those without a spout have a erect thumbpiece. Where the simple strap handle is used, the hinge and thumbpiece are fixed to the top of the handle but towards the end of the 18th century a scroll handle is used which is applied lower down the body. The cover hinge juts out from the lip rim and is quite separate from the handle. The style later reverted to the handle being applied at the lip. Another feature to look for is the junction of cover and body: whether the cover overlaps the rim or whether, as in later examples, the rim flares outwards to meet the protruding edge of the cover. The different alloys

A Leiden flagon of the 17th
century, 12¾in.

used in the late 18th century – primarily the greater use of
antimony – gives a greyer and lighter finish to some of these
flagons.

With few exceptions, it is often difficult to pinpoint the
area in which a piece was made, unless marks give assistance. One such example is the type of flagon made in
Leiden: here the belly of the piece is comparatively narrow
and rests on a high almost cylindrical lower section – there is
no foot or base as such. Amsterdam specialized in flagons
with a large capacity – quite a slender neck above a huge

A single-reeded dish, the border punched with initials and date.

bulbous body. One must of course be on the look-out for features crossing the borders; in Friesland we find similarities with northern Germany; flagons made in Cologne sometimes have features in common with those made in the Low Countries (particularly in the base); and others made in northeastern France, such as in Lille (once politically united with Belgium), closely resemble Flemish examples.

DISHES

Paintings show that up till the 16th century dishes were only used to bring in the food and were placed in the centre of the table – individual platters being made more often of wood. These large dishes were of the broad-rimmed type. In the 17th and 18th centuries, plates and dishes were similar to English broad-rimmed, single-reeded and plain-rimmed examples. Armorials were engraved in the centre or on the border of dishes. Initials were sometimes engraved on the border, but frequently punched, the punch often being a square or oval enclosing the initial. It was the custom, though not a definite rule, to punch three or four separate initials in a line. The metal used was hard and when cast was often strengthened by hammer blows on the reverse of the booge, although recent research suggests that not all pewter "work hardens" as was universally believed at this time. The rims were also strengthened by an overlap on the underside. A typically Dutch style emerged in the 18th century with, most typical of all, square dishes and salvers with waved rococo borders.

INKSTANDS

Alongside the group portraits of guild members which show their flagons, there are others of similar nature – of governors of various institutions. Once again these men are often grouped round a table but this is now laden with documents,

Above Inkstands of the 18th and early 19th centuries, each with provision for ink, pounce and quills, and two with drawers for wafers.

Left A pair of candlesticks made c. 1740, bearing traces of lacquering; 9¾in.

at the centre of which is, more often than not, a pewter inkstand with quill pen. The rectangular tray usually holds three detachable containers for ink, pens and pounce and underneath a tray for wafers. Another design was of upright rectangular form incorporating the inkwell (which had a hinged cover and a thumbpiece), and detachable pounce pot. In the 18th century a smaller type was also made of plain square bombé form which held two triangular containers centred by a quill hole. These were also made in the rococo style.

DOMESTIC PEWTER

Domestic pewter, such as salvers, candlesticks, wine coolers, tureens, chamber pots and medical instruments, cruets and coffee pots, was made in the prevailing styles of the silversmiths from the late 17th to early 19th centuries. Being a protestant country, the Netherlands received many fleeing French Huguenot craftsmen whose talents influenced style here, as elsewhere. The classical design of their work was adapted to native tastes and a Dutch style developed in domestic goods. The rococo style, too, was adapted but was less popular here than in Germany. Instead of moulded curves swirling round a piece, we see straight folds with the use of rocaille ornament limited to extremities – finials, feet and handles. Candlesticks and tea caddies were candidates for this style. Strangely though, while we think of the extremes of rococo as being too flamboyant for the Dutch, they did not object to the ornament of the neo-classical period. Indeed they developed floral swags, classical heads and piercing to such a degree of delicacy as to almost lose sight of the original inspiration. Inkstands, cruets and chestnut urns are examples to be found by the collector today.

The regular sea routes used by Dutch merchants in the 16th and 17th centuries extended to China, and tea was brought to the Low Countries in 1610. The opportunities for social gatherings afforded by the introduction of tea, coffee, chocolate and tobacco were recognized early and receptacles for them are the domestic items most commonly found today. Although they are nearly all late 18th- and early 19th-century, there were probably pewter teapots, coffee pots and tobacco jars made earlier which have not survived (the earliest known hallmarked English silver teapot is dated 1670). Tea and coffee urns are other pieces of household equipment which were made well into the 19th century, in various sizes. Some were made to the current fashions but a

A 19th-century coffee pot with wooden finial and shell thumbpiece (6¼in), and a coffee urn with brass tap, wooden finial and bun feet; c. 1800, and possibly German. 8¾in.

A fluted oval tobacco box; mid-18th century, 6¾ in high.

more usual style is pear-shaped with a domed cover and resting on three slender legs – high enough to leave room for a burner underneath. They sometimes have wooden feet, which conduct less heat. The tap which protrudes from the body is often made of brass. Originally many would have had a triangular stand – but stand and urn have usually been separated at some stage.

Tobacco jars are of casket form and should have a lead presser inside, although this has frequently been lost. Plain examples sometimes have a negro's head finial (as on some Swiss flagons, see p. 123), and another popular type was made in a straight-fold rococo style, of square or rectangular outline with simple vertical fluting enlivened by rocaille feet.

LACQUERING

A form of decoration which was popular on these items – and which was used on other articles such as candlesticks – was lacquering. The use of this highly coloured decoration transformed the original article; however, on many pieces seen today the lacquering has worn away. The theory that wares from the Low Countries were sent to Pontypool in Wales for japanning has been questioned.

Left A lacquered tea urn of
c. 1800, with an undecorated
stand of similar date.

Right Wrigglework engraving
of foliage, mostly tulips, on a
teapot and brandy bowl from
Friesland.

Below right Four porringers,
probably from the East Friesland area bordering Germany;
18th and 19th century, 9–12 in.

BRANDY BOWLS

The écuelle or porringer is often known in the Low Countries
as a brandy bowl. Outstanding among these are the type
made in Friesland. The bowl is engraved in wrigglework with
flowers and scrolling ornament and has two cast caryatid
handles. The body rests on a shallow pedestal foot. Further
south, in the 16th to 19th centuries, the porringer takes the
more usual plain form, with shaped ears either plain or
pierced, and sometimes applied in the bowl with a cast
rosette. Earlier deep bowls have simple ring handles.

LOW COUNTRIES

A pair of altar candlesticks, Dutch or northwest German; c. 1500.

SPOONS AND TOYS

Spoon makers were independent from other pewterers and spoon collecting is a special study. The simple round-bowled Dutch spoon, with cylindrical or flattened stem (chiefly made in Friesland) is perhaps the item most commonly found in general antique shops today. A lot of these are, however, reproductions made in this century. Styles varied little through the centuries, other examples having twisted stems, cone terminals or figure finials. They are usually marked inside the bowl.

Another popular area of collecting is toys. It is possible to find the whole range of domestic pewterware reproduced in miniature, sometimes in a doll's house, as in Germany (see p. 90).

CHURCH PEWTER

In the Low Countries as elsewhere there was a preference for using silver in churches; when pewter was used it usually conformed to the designs of contemporary gold-smiths and did not differ greatly from pieces made in other countries. This particularly applies to chalices, altar cruets, chrismatories and pyxes (though many early pieces descri-bed as such are in fact salts). However, the altar candlesticks made from the 15th to the late 17th century are particularly

A late 17th-century altar vase decorated in the lobed style brought by the Huguenots from France; 8in.

fine and similar examples are also found in Germany. The bases and drip-pans are usually of similar, though not identical, design – each tapering outwards, away from a central cylindrical and knopped stem. The drip-pans or sconces are centred by bold prickets which hold the candles. Pricket candlesticks continued to be made for churches well into the 17th and early 18th centuries, although their form became lighter.

Alongside the candlesticks stood altar vases; a typical late 17th-century example, with the lobed decoration which had spread with the Huguenots from France, is illustrated. This style is also found in Germany.

In Protestant churches we find communion beakers, particularly in the 17th century. The plain tapering style conforms with those made in silver. Beakers of this type were also made for engraving commemorative scenes and inscriptions.

Jewish ritual pewter should also be mentioned here, although stylistically it differs little from its German counter-parts. The rococo style, for example, was used to decorate hanukah lamps (see p. 43). The basic shape of seder dishes was the same as a secular piece and it is only the engraving which distinguishes them.

SCANDINAVIA

With the exception of a handful of pieces in relief and some Hanseatic jugs (mentioned earlier on p. 16) very little Scandinavian pewter prior to the 17th century survives. However, as elsewhere, a fairly wide range of items can still be seen from the 18th century onwards. Scandinavian pewterers were scattered throughout the region, importing tin from England and Germany. The major centres of production in Denmark were Copenhagen, Viborg and Aalborg and in Norway Bergen, Trondheim, Stavanger and Christiana or Oslo. In Sweden the busiest towns for pewter making were Stockholm, Göteborg, Jönköping, Karlskrona and Uppsala, but pewter was made in about fifty other centres of varying importance. Mr Birger Bruzelli has calculated that government records show an output of approximately 6,000,000 items of pewter in Sweden between 1754 and 1914.

The histories of Denmark, Finland, Norway and Sweden are so closely linked that the affinity of their pewter can come as no surprise. The proximity of Baltic towns along the north German coast, some of which later fell under Swedish control (for example Bremen, Reval or Tallinn, Riga) also has a direct influence on the design of much Scandinavian pewter.

In 1397 Denmark, Norway and Sweden (including Finland) formed the Kalmar Union under the Danish queen Margaret. This did not prevent frequent wars between Denmark and Sweden, however, and the union was dissolved in 1523. Finland remained Swedish territory and Norway (which had been allied with Denmark since the 14th century) was incorporated under the Danish monarchy. The turbulent

Cylindrical measures from Copenhagen; 19th century. The narrow band of moulding, simple scroll handle and stunted erect thumbpiece are characteristic.

FINLAND

Umeälven

Trondheim

NORWAY

SWEDEN

Klarälven

GULF OF
BOTHNIA

L
Ladoga

Vyborg

Bergen

Oslo
(Christiania)

Uppsala

Turku
(Abo)

Helsinki
(Helsingfors)

Stavanger

Stockholm

Tallinn (Reval)
ESTONIA

Nyköping

LIVONIA

Christiansand

Göteborg

Jonköping

Riga

NORTH SEA

Aalborg

Viborg

DENMARK

Copenhagen

Karlskrona

Dvina

Malmö

BALTIC SEA

Kiel

SCHLESWIG-
HOLSTEIN

Lübeck

Rostock

Kaliningrad
(Königsberg)

Bremen

Hamburg

Elbe

Oder

Szczecin
(Stettin)

Gdansk
(Danzig)

Wisla

| 0 | | 200mi |
| 0 | | 250km |

Scandinavia, north Germany and the Baltic and their chief centres of pewter production.

years of the 17th century, specifically 1628–1709, during which so much of Europe was in the midst of political and social upheaval, were the years of Sweden's greatest power under such rulers as Gustavus Adolphus, his daughter Christina and, on her abdication, Charles x. In 1809 Finland was handed to Russia, who had been steadily increasing her influence there ever since the decline of Swedish power (Finland obtained independence in 1917) and in 1814 Denmark lost Norway to Sweden (their union survived to 1905). Wars between Denmark and Germany over Schleswig-Holstein were resolved in Germany's favour in 1866 and as late as 1937 Lübeck, which had been self-governing since 1226 and as the leading Hanseatic port had acted as buffer between Germany and Scandinavia, lost her free status.

TANKARDS AND MEASURES

Sets of measures, in sizes, were produced throughout Scandinavia. Danish and Norwegian examples of the 18th and 19th centuries are cylindrical with a narrow band of moulding at the foot and lip. The smallest sizes are usually without handles, the larger sizes having simple scroll handles of strap form with a rather stunted erect thumbpiece. Some examples have a flat lid and the thumbpiece is then of the Germanic ridged type, placed over the hinge. Swedish measures were made in five sizes. Their shape is of very slightly tapering form on a projecting moulded base and, unlike the Danish and Norwegian measures, the Swedish measures have a spout. The scroll handle has a ridged terminal and is surmounted at the cover hinge by an erect or plumed thumbpiece. Another type of Swedish measure is of steeply tapering form with a small scroll handle below a cut-away rim.

The link with northern Germany is seen in cylindrical flagons and tankards made throughout Scandinavia from the 17th century. Of varying size, they rest on moulded skirt or flat bases and have flat-topped domed covers. Thumbpieces are usually variants of the ball type; handles are scrolled with

A tapering spouted flagon of the kind made in quantity in the 18th and 19th centuries in Scandinavia; 8¾in.

A coin set into the domed lid is a distinctive feature of many Scandinavian tankards. This Swedish tankard is by Eric Almquist, of Eskilstuna; c. 1850, 8½in.

Above left A tankard engraved with wrigglework, on pomegranate feet; *right* a tankard by Marcus Pedersen Brandt of Bergen, mid 18th century; both 7½in; *centre* a Swedish spouted measure dated 1822; 8½in.

Below A Norwegian tankard, probably by Peder Mads Vahl of Bergen; 18th century, 7½in. The flattened sphere of the ball thumbpiece is a Scandinavian feature.

ridged terminals. Rörken (German examples are described on p. 99) were also made in Scandinavia and, with only minor stylistic changes, continued to be made throughout the 19th century, sometimes inlaid with copper or brass.

The influence of the Low Countries is seen in Norwegian spouted flagons. Some of these are extensively decorated with bands encircling the body, a form of decoration which had been in use since the 15th century.

Silver designs of the late 17th and 18th centuries are repeated in pewter in cylindrical tankards on three feet and with matching thumbpiece. These feet are usually claw-and-ball or embossed in baroque taste with bold foliage or are in the form of a pomegranate. The plain body is decorated at the feet and handle with similar motifs.

The two types of measure which are probably those most frequently seen today are cylindrical, and tapering spouted. Both were made with only slight stylistic differences for most of the 18th and 19th centuries. The average height of these measures is 8in. They were often decorated with wrigglework engraving. The plain lines of the tapering spouted measures are sometimes decorated with two broad bands of moulded girdles. Features common to both types are ball or fluted thumbpieces and handles of either scroll or double-scroll form. This latter style of handle was introduced in the 18th century and is very similar to that seen in English mugs and tankards, although the Scandinavian form is rather more pronounced. In Finland the gap between the fishtail terminal and the kink in the scroll is sometimes almost closed.

165

Rococo soup tureen from Holstein, with spiral lobes; mid-18th century, 14in.

A very distinctive feature of Scandinavian tankards of every type is that a coin or medal is frequently inset into the lid – cylindrical tankards of the late 18th and 19th centuries make a pronounced feature of this, the cover rising in a steep dome to the central coin or medallion. The symmetrical erect thumbpiece of German origin developed in the early 19th century into a slightly flared fluted form, bent backwards towards the handle. The ball thumbpiece either copied its German counterpart or, from the 17th century, took a more local form in which the sphere is flattened and flows into its stem.

DOMESTIC PEWTER
From the mid-18th century a large proportion of domestic pewter was made in rococo, then neo-classical, followed by Empire styles. The items which seemed most suited to rococo were candlesticks, tureens, sauceboats, teapots and coffee pots. Many of these were of fine quality, and the style continued to be used as late as 1800, long after it had ceased to be fashionable. Neo-classicism was well-suited to small covered bowls with high loop handles, the body sometimes applied with plaquettes, and also to candlesticks. of which a high proportion are still in existence. A popular form of candlestick of the 1780s and 1790s was square-based, sometimes with four ball feet, the base rising and tapering towards the column stem and sconce. Small candlesticks eliminated the stem and the sconce rested on the base. Borders were decorated with lobing, husk festoons, piercing

Right A tureen from Aalborg, Denmark, with vertical lobing, drop-ring handles, wooden finial and claw-and-ball feet; 1746, 12½in.

Below right A dish by Hans Høy of Copenhagen; 1834

or beading – features which continued to the 1820s, by which time the rather more severe Empire fashion developed, incorporating classical motifs, lyres, stiff leafage and anthemions. In the 19th century teapots and coffee pots were rather plain, made in varying styles with no very distinctive features.

Beakers once again follow contemporary silver styles, being of flared tapering form, with a moulded base. As the 18th century progressed the flare of the body became more pronounced. The body is sometimes left plain, sometimes decorated with engraved wrigglework.

SCANDINAVIA

PLATES AND DISHES

Plates and dishes followed the conventional patterns of other countries to a large extent. Marks were placed on the border or on the underside in the centre of the plate. Broad rims in the 17th century were followed by single-reeded rims in the early 18th century. Also, of course, in the 18th century wavy-edged and plain-rimmed plates were made. All these designs were also applied to oval serving dishes. The beaded border was also popular, the roundels being slightly larger and spaced further apart than, for example, the English beaded plate.

An earlier type of plate, made in Denmark from the 17th century, was of octagonal form with bold roundels at intervals on the border. This very distinctive form has a broad rim which, in the late 17th century is sometimes also engraved with foliage.

BOWLS

Covered dishes for serving food tended to follow the German and French forms, the use of drop-ring handles being popular. However a typically Scandinavian feature is the form of handle illustrated, the upwards and outwards thrust of the handles resembling the prow of a viking ship. This comparison is most noticeable in the handles in the form of birds' heads, but others have pomegranates or simple moulding. The form of bowl is usually compressed circular, either on a moulded skirt base or three ball feet, the body either plain or decorated with bold lobing. Some bowls have covers with finials matching the feet (seen also on the Swiss *Wochnerinnenschüssel*, for example) so that they can be used as plates.

There are two more types of bowl native to Scandinavia.

A covered bowl with relief-decorated handle and front grip; 7¾in. These bowls were also made in north Germany.

168

Right A two-handled bowl from Jönköping, c. 1820. The handles are typically Scandinavian in form.

Below right An octagonal Danish plate with bold roundels at the angles; late 17th century, 11½in.

First, a brandy bowl (porringer or écuelle) with flat beaded ring handle, sometimes with another handle opposite of a different form, either pierced triangular or a moulded shell. The body of these simple and functional items is usually left plain.

Another type of bowl comes from Norway, although similar examples are also found in north Germany. The compressed circular body rests on a spreading skirt base and has a hinged domed cover usually centred by a finial. The hinge and thumbpiece top a simple scroll handle, the terminal of which sometimes extends to the level of the base to prevent the bowl falling over backwards when the cover is opened. Opposite this handle is another, in the form of a grip, enabling the user to hold the bowl with both hands.

UNITED STATES OF AMERICA

The American pewter which is available to the present-day collector comes almost exclusively from the period 1750–1850. Due to this relatively short time-span and the rarity of pre-1750 pewter a large proportion of American pewter seen today is Britannia metal. This chapter discusses 19th-century work, including Britannia metal, whereas a separate chapter is devoted to European pewter of the same period.

The large quantity of pewter in America can roughly be divided into three categories: pieces which bear marks of American makers, those which bear English marks, and unmarked pewter, the majority of which could have been made either side of the Atlantic, unless it exhibits a combination of features from various European countries that bespeaks adaptation to the American taste. By the beginning of the 19th century the use of traditional pewter casting methods was on the wane; the successor, Britannia metal, continued to be popular until the Civil War, after which it was used chiefly as a base for electroplating.

Throughout the second half of the 17th century a steady flow of immigrants arrived to start life afresh in the colonies. Although most settlers were English, the Dutch settled in New Amsterdam – renamed New York after its capture by the English in 1664 – and German and Swedish settlers joined the English in Pennsylvania. British mercantile policies were based on ideas of England and the colonies working together as a unit, not competing but rather complementing one another. In many respects this hampered growth in America, for it discouraged manufacture there in favour of building up a large export trade for Britain. By the end of the 18th century, after more than a century of steady population increase and development of industry, trade and agriculture, the colonists were still being restrained by the English, and "taxation without representation" became a major source of friction. During the War of Independence (1775–83) a considerable amount of pewter was probably melted to help in the war, for example in making bullets. Afterwards, the east coast remained the commercial and industrial centre of the country. The making of pewter was confined to this area, Cincinnati being the westernmost town of any importance where pewter or Britannia metal was made.

When the first colonists arrived they brought with them only basic supplies, but this changed as experience of what was needed was relayed to England for the benefit of new emigrants, many of whom were more prosperous than their predecessors. Pewter was included amongst household requisites, as well as wooden utensils. As early as 1635 a pewterer, Richard Graves, is recorded as having a shop in Salem, Massachusetts. But by 1700 there was still only a handful of known pewterers, in Virginia, Pennsylvania, Maryland and Massachusetts. All came from England.

The East Coast of North America and the towns of most important pewter manufacture. Although most pewterers, and most imported pewter, came from England, the influence of other settlers, from Germany, the Low Countries and Sweden, has also been important.

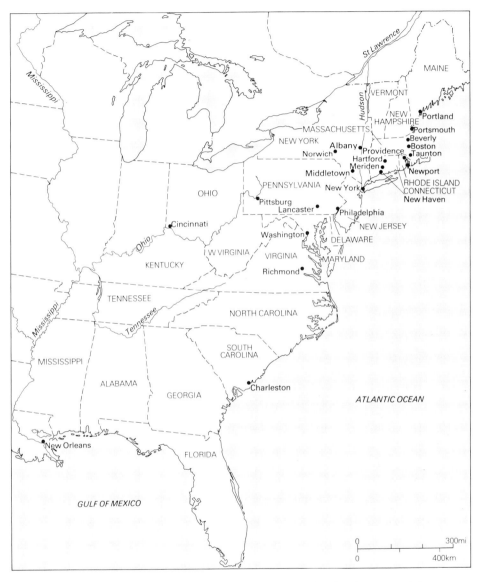

The major influence on the development of the pewter trade in the 17th and 18th centuries was British law. The export of pure tin to British colonies was prohibited; there was no tax on imported finished articles, but for many years there was a high duty on unworked pewter brought into north America. The American pewterers therefore had to rely almost entirely on the repairing of pewter and on the

171

chance to rework pewter obtained by melting old and worn-out pieces brought in by customers. This meant that most pewterers ran a shop and sold wares imported from England alongside their own. By 1725 towns such as Boston, New York and Philadelphia each supported several pewterer's shops. Usually the pewterer could sell his own goods at considerably lower prices than those by his English competitors and yet there was such cachet attached to the imported article that at times he had difficulty in persuading people to buy his own pieces. English pewter was renowned for its quality, and one of the American pewterer's hardest tasks was to maintain standards. He had to test the content of pieces he melted, some of which were probably made by local tinkers or had been brought by settlers from Germany, Holland or Sweden and so contained different proportions of lead in the alloy. And of course the pewterer in America had immense difficulty in obtaining pure tin to upgrade the alloy where necessary.

In America in the 18th century those who could not afford pewter still used wooden utensils and cheap earthenware. Porcelain was not seen in any large quantity until around the end of the century. The amount of pewter exported from England, especially by the London and Bristol pewterers, was enormous and it increased throughout the 18th century. Shipments were quantified by weight as well as number of objects; by 1760 approximately 300 tons a year were sent from England to the value of £38,000. By and large the quality of exported British pewter was good, with notable exceptions such as plates by the Bristol maker Allen Bright which were certainly made of inferior quality alloy with as much as 30% lead. More pewter was imported than any other domestic ware. Even after the Revolution the trade with England continued. In 1784, for example, the English Quaker pewterer John Townsend combined his business and religious interests by going on a preaching tour of America, selling his pewter as he went. By the early 19th century England was exporting pieces commemorating the Revolution.

Pewterers who emigrated brought moulds with them from England and Germany but soon began to make their own and so develop an individual style, the basis of which was English. Throughout the 18th century the pieces made in America mirror the dishes, mugs and tankards of England. Often they are many years behind the current English fashions and, even though a new style was adopted, the old styles continued to be made. Thus tankards of an English style of 1700 were still being made at the end of the 18th century. There are, of course, regional differences in style and also in the popularity of certain items in any area, some of which are noted later in this chapter.

The banner of the Society of Pewterers of New York City. It was carried in the Federal Procession on 23 July, 1788, to celebrate ratification of the Constitution of the United States. The "coat-of-arms" is blazoned with a distiller's worm, a common product in pewter, and besides the two spouted vessels a teapot

which is repeated in the group of contemporary vessels on a shelf. Below is a pewterer's shop with workmen hammering a large dish, turning the drive-wheel of a lathe, working on a vessel on the lathe, and in the corner pouring moulten pewter from a big ladle into a mould.

The tradition of the guild system was not transferred across the Atlantic. On the whole regulations regarding the quality of pewter were not as strict as in England. Nevertheless, an apprentice system was established and pewterers formed societies. The banner of the New York Society of Pewterers not only illustrates pewter which was fashionable at the time the banner was made (1788) but also a scene of four men at work, one turning a lathe for his colleague, another working on a dish and a fourth working at the back of the workshop.

UNITED STATES OF AMERICA

MAKERS

The best known American pewterer is most probably William Will. His father, John, who emigrated from Neuwied in Germany to New York in 1752, was also a pewterer, and obviously realized that his English clientele would not feel familiar with and therefore would not buy pieces which bore any resemblance to those of his native Rhineland and his work, notably tankards and mugs, became almost completely Anglicized. He continued to work in New York from the time of his arrival until about 1774. By this time his sons Henry, Philip and William had followed him into the trade. Henry Will worked for a time in New York City and also in Albany. Philip, after completing his apprenticeship in New York moved to Philadelphia – by then the largest and richest town of the whole colony. William Will also moved to Philadelphia in 1764 and stayed until his death in 1798. In those 30 years he probably made a greater variety of vessels than any other maker and also a very large quantity. He also maintained a high standard of craftsmanship. Will was the only pewterer who attempted to keep pace with European fashion rather than being content to produce pieces which were years out of date. This is most apparent in his teapots, flagons and coffee pots in the neo-classical style.

Another maker of German birth was Johann Christoph Heyne (1715–81) who worked in Lancaster, Pennsylvania. Heyne altered his style to suit the customer – thus for most domestic pewter made for English settlers he adopted the English style, but when making pieces for the German Lutheran church the influence of his homeland is paramount. He is perhaps best known for his ecclesiastical pewter because of its distinctive blending of German and English design.

Next to the Will family, pewter made by the Bassetts probably has the highest reputation amongst collectors. Their work spans the whole of the 18th century, ending exactly in 1800 with the death of Frederick Bassett. Frederick (1740–1800) and his elder brother Francis (born 1729) were two sons of John Basset (1696–1761) who, with his first cousin Francis I (1690–1758) continued the trade which their grandfather John Bassett had brought to the colonies early in the 17th century. The Bassetts worked in New York and made tankards, mugs and dishes of a consistently high standard and good quality of metal.

But the family whose work surpasses all in quantity, if not in quality, is the Danforths. They built up a very substantial business producing enormous quantities of pewter to a consistent quality but not the finest. Their work contained a high proportion of lead, as did that of many pewterers outside the major towns. Members of the family and their apprentices were dispersed throughout the country; their

A pair of tulip-shaped beakers by Israel Trask; 5¾in.

history begins with Thomas Danforth, who began work in Taunton, Massachusetts in 1727. His elder son, Thomas II, moved to Middletown, Connecticut where five of his sons began work, as did two grandsons. Thomas I's other son, John, worked in Norwich, Connecticut and was also followed in the trade by his son and grandson. Just as important, though, is the fact that his daughter married Oliver Boardman. Their three children continued to work in Litchfield and Hartford, Connecticut, Thomas Danforth Boardman and Sherman Boardman eventually going into partnership with Lucius Hart (Boardman and Hart).

Britannia metal was first manufactured in England about 1770. Thomas Danforth Boardman was the first to experiment with the new alloy in America and began to produce teapots around 1805–6. The alloy gave a new lease of life to the trade for it was possible to make a far greater range of objects in Britannia metal, more cheaply and in fashionable and popular styles. This expansion coincided with the opening of the west and an enormous population explosion. Between 1790 and 1820 the population doubled to 9½ million and the new families needed domestic wares.

A maker who understood design and decoration of such objects because of his previous work as a silversmith was Israel Trask (1786–1867), who lived in Beverly, Massachusetts. Other important names in the manufacture of Britannia metal are, for example, Reed and Barton of Taunton, Mass., whose business was founded in 1840. A few years earlier in the same town the Taunton Britannia Manufacturing Co. operated between 1830 and 1834. In West Meriden, Connecticut, were the Meriden Britannia Co., and Roswell Gleason, who saw the Britannia metal trade through to its close and retired in 1871.

PORRINGERS
Whereas nearly all English porringers date from before 1750, it is only from that date onwards that American porringers are found today, most of them being 19th century. They were used for eating and drinking and were made in various sizes (including miniatures). When the spoon was the most common utensil, knives being in short supply, the deep bowl of the porringer was more practical for some meals than the plate. A lot of porringers were made in New England (notably Rhode Island). There was also demand for them in New York and Pennsylvania, with the notable exception of Philadelphia.

Stylistically there are two types of bowl, those with the flat base and those with a central boss, but the principal feature

Porringers, the handles derived from English designs; two have a central boss in the base, the base of the other is of the flat type. *Top* by William Kirby, New York; *centre* by John Basset; *bottom* by Richard Lee Sr. or Jr., Springfield, Vermont; mid to late 18th century.

Left Two porringers with decorated cast handles from Providence, Rhode Island; *left* c.1817–56 by William Calder; *right* 1774–1809 by Gershom Jones (1774–1809).

Right Porringers with plain handles; *left* c. 1796 probably by Thomas Melville for David Melville, Newport, Rhode Island; *right* by Thomas Danforth III, early 19th century.

Below right Beaker by Boardman and Hart, 3¾in; plate by Thomas Danforth III, 8in; candlesticks by Henry Hopper in New York, 10in; bowl (with indistinct marks), 11½in. All 1st half 19th century.

is the single handle or "ear", on which is usually struck the maker's touch. Of the many different varieties, those with decoratively pierced handles (scrolls, hearts, triangles, rect-angles, the more elaborate with dolphins and/or a crown) derive from the 17th- and 18th-century English and 18th-century north German examples, whereas plain handles may be influenced by late 18th- and 19th-century French examples. The handles were cast directly onto the piece, rather than soldered on (as in reproductions and fakes), except for Pennsylvanian porringers with plain "tab" handles, which are all cast complete in one mould.

PLATES, DISHES AND BASINS
The early explorers and settlers used wooden plates. Later, in the lists of pewter exported from England, plates and dishes usually formed the major part of each consignment. However, because of wear and tear they were probably the article which had to be replaced most frequently. The majority of American plates and dishes are of single-reeded type; the plain-rimmed form was less popular. Plates varied in size between 7in and 10in. For dishes 16in was, with very

Two quart tankards of the late 18th/early 19th centuries, *left* by William Will, *right* by Parks Boyd of Philadelphia.

rare exceptions, the maximum diameter. Regional differences are found principally in the size favoured — 11in and 13in dishes were made in Connecticut but not dishes as large as 15in or 16in. Boston, for example, favoured small, narrow-rimmed shallow plates. Plates and dishes of the same diameter also varied in weight, and they were usually sold by weight.

Like plates and dishes, deep bowls or basins were made in graded sizes, usually with a single band of moulding at the narrow rim. Some makers struck their touch inside the centre of the bowl. They may have been influenced in this practice by Scottish makers such as Stephen Maxwell or Graham and Wardrop, both of Glasgow, whose sympathies were clearly indicated by their touches, inscribed respectively "May y United States of America flourish" and "Success to the United States of America". Others placed their mark on the reverse, in the manner more customary for marking plates and dishes.

TANKARDS

Cider and beer were the drinks for which tankards were most popularly used. Although the form of tankards is based on English examples, it is always interesting to see how details are borrowed which subtly alter the character of a piece and perhaps betray the original nationality of its maker — for example by the addition of a finial reminiscent of a crested tappit-hen, the dome typical of a Scandinavian tankard, or engraved initials in the Germanic rather than the English style (p. 34). Unlike mugs, tankards did not survive the transition to Britannia metal and were not made after around 1800. Right up to this date some pewterers continued to make styles by then 50 or 80 years out of date by English standards. Flat-topped tankards were a speciality of New York pewterers; Philadelphia makers, on the other hand (notably William Will); preferred the baluster or tulip shape which was first seen in England around 1725 but was at the height of its popularity in Bristol c. 1750–90. One feature in common use was the scroll handle, variations showing in the terminal — for example spade, fishtail or ball.

MUGS

Mugs or cans (this nowadays an American rather than an English term) were widely used throughout the east coast and were made chiefly in pint and quart capacities. One type of mug rarely seen is barrel-shaped, and the most popular shape was tapering cylindrical. Stylistic differences are found in the angle of the body and in the placing of moulded girdles; late examples have incised bands. Once again, the most frequently used handle is the simple scroll with ball terminal, often topped with an attractively moulded

Left to right Plate with corded border by James H. Putnam of Malden, early 19th century, 5¼in, and plate by Nathaniel Austin of Charlestown, late 18th century, 8in, both in Massachusetts; dish by Frederick Bassett, 13½in; bowl c. 1830–35 by Thomas Danforth III, with eagle and "TD" stamped on bottom; 9in.

Left A quart tankard by Frederick Bassett; 6⅞in. The design is based on English examples of the late 17th and early 18th centuries (see pp. 58–9.

Right A rare mug with "moon-face" handle terminal; 4½in, Boston, mid-18th century. Previously attributed to John Skinner; recent research by Mr W. O. Blaney suggests John Bonynge as the maker, though both pewterers may have used the same moulds.

thumbgrip of various design. A less common handle was the double-scroll or "broken" handle, which was also applied to tulip-shaped mugs. In New England (where mugs were made in large quantities, the tankard apparently being unpopular) pewterers developed the strap handle – a type known in earlier English mugs. Nathaniel Austin incorporated his name in the handle terminal and an attractive shell motif at the top. Other makers placed marks beside the handle or on the inside of the base, and in the 19th century on the underside of the piece.

BEAKERS, FLAGONS AND CHURCH PEWTER

The communion pewter illustrated is part of a set of 12 beakers, 2 flagons, 2 basins and 2 plates. This is a fairly typical example of an extensive set which might have belonged to any New England church. The same design of beaker, plate or flagon was used for home or tavern as for religious use.

The most usual design of 18th-century beaker is comparable to Dutch beakers, of tall tapering form, flared at the lip and with a moulded base. Later squatter examples are more English in feeling. In the 19th century a short bell-shaped bowl on a rim or pedestal foot became popular; this was made in Britannia metal in large numbers.

Flagons made after 1750 were made almost exclusively for church use. The most normal basic type was of tall tapering cylindrical form with a domed lid, but of all the objects made in America in pewter the most individual are most probably the flagons. Single examples of a particular style of flagon are often all that is known, particularly for the 18th century. In the flagon, even more than the tankard,

Part of a communion set (there is also a fitted container), bearing various marks of Danforth and Boardman, late 18th century.

were united characteristics of Scandinavian, German and English traditions. Chalices too, show great variety in the shape of the bowl and stem. Outstanding among these flagons and chalices are pieces made by members of the Will family and by Johann Cristoph Heyne. (Heyne and other makers sometimes used a plate to form the base of a flagon. This practice was sometimes copied in the 20th century in the making of fake English flagons. The prospective buyer should look for knife scratches, which are usually a fair indication of such copying.)

PITCHERS

Here again, terminology can sometimes cause confusion. Just as in Europe the term "measure" is sometimes hard to define, in America the problem lies with "flagon" and "pitcher". As has already been stated, the majority of 18th century flagons were made for ecclesiastical use rather than for serving drink in the home. At the end of the 18th century Parks Boyd made a covered water pitcher of convex form with a short spout and scroll handle. This shape developed into the pitchers, both lidded and unlidded, made by many of the Britannia metal manufacturers, and based on cream

A covered pitcher by Boardman and Co., New York; c. 1820, 8in.

UNITED STATES OF AMERICA

ware jugs from Liverpool. These are baluster, with a short rim foot and scroll handle; the short spout follows the contours of the body. The domed covers are centred by a finial.

Smaller pitchers for milk or cream follow very closely designs of English silver, both 18th-century examples and 19th-century Britannia metal pieces.

TEAPOTS AND COFFEE POTS
Milk and cream pitchers in the 19th century came to be an integral part of the "tea and coffee set". In the 18th century these items were not made in sets as such. However in the 19th century a typical four-piece set would include teapot, coffee pot, milk jug and sugar basin. Because it was not practical to use a burner (which would melt the pewter) it was obviously not possible to make tea kettles in pewter. Chocolate pots do not appear to have been made on either side of the Atlantic, nor are there any known surviving English coffee pots of the first half of the 18th century.

The typical style for the American 18th-century teapot was based on the "Queen Anne" style silver pots of pear-shaped outline with a high domed cover and gently curved spout; some rest on three feet. Their most prolific maker was William Will, who went on to make neo-classical style

Above A cream pitcher, c. 1780, possibly Philadelphia; 4in.

Below Miniature porringer (?Richard Lee, Sr. or Jr., 1747–1823, b. 1775), 2½in; sundial, 3in; miniature "pigeon-breasted" teapot (?Roswell Gleason); shaving dish (?A. Griswold, 1784–1853).

Right A coffee pot c. 1790 by William Will, 16in, and one c. 1815 by Israel Trask, 11½in.

pots in the 1780s and 1790s concurrently with his coffee pots and flagons. Once Will died, the market was wide open for other makers, and the advent of Britannia metal expanded the possibilities further. By the 1830s there was a wide range of teapots and coffee pots, most of them being various forms of baluster. One of the most popular has come to be called "pigeon-breasted".

CANDLESTICKS AND LAMPS

American candlesticks made before 1830 are rare. Those made in Britannia metal usually have baluster or V-shaped stems resting on a domed circular base. These were adapted into a chamberstick style by replacing the base with a dished pan with side handle.

Items which have a greater interest to the American collector are the lamps, made in vast quantities between 1820 and 1870. Early examples were made to burn whale oil or burning fluid (alcohol and turpentine). These had one or two cylinders containing wicks which protruded from the fuel container (called the font). There was a wide range of styles for table use and also swinging lamps, which could either be hung on a wall or placed flat on a table. Another

Top A pear-shaped teapot; early 19th century, 7½in.

Above A covered sugar bowl with beaded borders; late 18th century, probably by William Will; 45/8in.

Left A coffee pot by Samuel Simpson of New York; c. 1790, 11¼in.

Right, above A pair of chamber candlesticks by Roswell Gleason, 19th century, 4¾in. *Below* A group of 19th-century lamps; the tallest (8in) is by William Calder of Providence, Rhode Island; the others are from 1½ to 4in high.

Left A double bull's-eye lamp of the type patented by Roswell Gleason; 19th century, 7½in.

Above, top to bottom Puritan round-bowl spoon, 1767–98, by William J. Elsworth, New York City, 7in; eagle and 12 stars, c. 1800–1840, probably by James or John Yates of Birmingham, England; neo-classical, c. 1790–1810, by George Coldwell, N.Y.C.; another fiddle-back handle, with "P. Derr 1820" on back; neo-classical with flat handle (the back, not shown, has a rococo scroll on the bowl) by William Will; neo-classical, with urn, 1800–1850; trefid end, 1690–1720 marked "I B S", American or English.

type is the grease lamp, which has wide slotted wick holders of rectangular form. One of the largest manufacturers of lamps was the Meriden Britannia Co., founded in 1852 when lamps were being produced in greater quantities than at any other time. Roswell Gleason was another maker of lamps and his firm manufactured the "bull's-eye" lamp, which incorporated glass to reflect and magnify the light.

These lamps, together with teasets, became the life-blood of the pewter trade. When their popularity ceased around 1870, the trade died.

SPOONS

Of all the many other articles made in pewter and Britannia metal, the most numerous were undoubtedly spoons. Precisely because they were such an important part of daily life, it is very rare to find spoons today which are pre-1800. The constant use wore them down or broke them. However there is no such shortage of spoons from the period 1830–70, although those which survive are probably only a fraction of the many thousands made. A few examples of the many different types are illustrated.

THE NINETEENTH CENTURY

Until recently in every field of the arts the 19th century has been something of an enigma. It has been rejected as an era of stylistic revivals when mechanization destroyed craft and when nothing of any merit was produced. Luckily these opinions have now been abandoned by most people as knowledge of the period increases and interest in its artefacts widens. Pewter has not escaped this attitude and has suffered more than most because it was a period of steady decline in the trade in the face of competition from other materials and because of changes in the composition of the metal which have been the cause of much confusion among collectors.

In order to understand these changes we must look back to the middle of the 18th century. The composition of pewter was altered continually as pewterers experimented with new techniques and tried to meet the demands of their customers for durable pieces which would not damage too easily. These changes are particularly noticeable in the 18th century when, as the marks tell us (p. 238), plates of "hard metal" or "superfine hard metal" became increasingly popular. As competition with pottery and porcelain became more intense, this use of hard metal spread to wares such as salts, coffee pots and teapots, although softer alloys continued to be used also.

The natural sequel to this gradual evolution of hard metal was an alloy developed in about 1769 by James Vickers of Sheffield which came to be known as "hard metal" or "Britannia metal". It consisted chiefly of tin and antimony but also contained very small quantities of copper and bismuth. These last were soon omitted, leaving an alloy of approximately 90% tin and 10% antimony. Its use led to a split in the pewter trade between those who developed the full potential of the new alloy and created factories producing large quantities of machine-made objects (which are termed "Britannia metal") and those who continued to work in the traditional way using hard alloys for plates and tableware and softer alloys for pub mugs and other hollow-ware. Britannia metal was amenable to different production methods (e.g. spinning) and the fact that less metal needed to be used made it much cheaper: manufacturers hoped to regain some of the market which pewter had lost by taking advantage of Britannia metal's adaptability to use mass-production methods.

The division in the trade did not last long. By about 1860–70 the trade had declined to such an extent that many of the large firms closed down (as in America) and others were drastically reduced in size. By this time the smaller "traditional" pewterers were making little other than hollow-ware and were no longer using such a variety of alloys: the old soft metal had virtually disappeared and hard metal alloys were

The trade card of James Brown, "manufacturer of all kinds of Britannia Metal goods, plated and compostion cruet and liquor frames, inkstands, & & &, Paradise Street, Birmingham". The predominance of contemporary silver over traditional pewter designs can clearly be seen.

used throughout the trade. Traditional alloys were no longer considered desirable. As people became more health conscious, lead was used in ever-decreasing quantities and in order to make use of modern technology it was necessary to use the new compositions. The composition of the hard metal marketed as pewter for the last 100 years is the result of centuries of development, of which Britannia metal was the penultimate phase. The split in the trade was healed as the pewterers closed ranks in order to survive.

James Vickers' discovery came at a time when Sheffield plate was being produced in ever-increasing quantities for an expanding market. Silver wares were available to less prosperous families than previously and resulted in further encroachments into the pewterers' territory. Moreover, the advantages and great potential of mechanization were beginning to be understood. At his Soho factory in Birmingham, Matthew Boulton went into partnership with James Watt to produce steam engines, and silversmiths such as the Batemans in London used Boulton's machinery in order to produce cheaper goods which could compete with the plate works of Sheffield. The properties of Britannia metal were such that it, too, could be rolled by heavy machinery. Alternatively, in the early days of Britannia metal, the entire piece was sometimes cast, using the same methods as for the

Above An imported Chinese tea caddy decorated profusely with foliage and birds; c. 1900.

Left A lidded baluster jug, mass-produced in thin-guage metal and hence easily damaged. The solder-line between the two halves can clearly be seen along the apex of the baluster.

traditional alloys. Pear-shaped teapots are perhaps the most commonly found examples of this method. Spinning was introduced, taking advantage of the fact that thin sheets of metal, after being cut into shape, could be turned on a lathe. Additional parts, such as handles, feet or spouts, were cast or stamped. Spinning really revolutionized the trade, and the method was continually improved and expanded.

But the major disadvantage of spinning lay in what was also its chief asset: cheapness. It led frequently to poor design and low standards of production. The smaller quantity of metal which needed to be used resulted in much lighter objects. The stress in the metal in component parts of a piece, due to poor workmanship, often caused a piece to buckle. It is these aspects of the trade which have been foremost in the minds of many pewter collectors causing them to spurn all Britannia metal. Nevertheless, well-designed pieces of good quality were also made, and it is these which the modern collectors should seek.

British manufacturers soon began exporting Britannia metal and the formula was worked out elsewhere. Although in England and America the alloy was known chiefly as Britannia metal, it was also know as "hard metal", "white metal" or "French metal". Thomas Danforth Boardman was the first to experiment with the alloy in America, and Britannia metal also spread to the rest of Europe. It was some time before its use was widespread; indeed it had taken some thirty years after James Vickers' first attempts for large-scale manufacture to take place in England. John Vickers, John Wolstenholme and Philip Ashberry were amongst the earliest manufacturers, but it was James Dixon, who established his factory in Sheffield in 1804, who was to lead the field for the rest of the century.

An English flagon of the "African jug" type, probably by Gaskell and Chambers; 11½in.

Above A jelly mould, a compressed circular salt cellar and a faceted milk jug. Jelly moulds were made in a multitude of shapes and sizes, some hinged, some (like this one) unscrewing.

Left An octagonal baluster coffee pot, 1st half 19th century.

John Culme in his book *Nineteenth Century Silver* quotes a short history of the firm of J. Dixon and Sons written for the *Jeweller and Metalworker* in 1889: "Mr James Dixon, the founder of the firm, made his name originally in the closing days of the last century by the bold and brilliant stroke of manufacturing in Britannia metal teapots and similar articles which up to that period had been produced only in the costly sterling plate or the brittle crockery ware. In 1804 Mr James Dixon with a Mr Smith commenced business and secured Cornish Place, which had been a rolling mill, and which was one of the few places where steam power was available. At this time the teapots made were mostly of oblong or oval forms, the bodies being stamped in two pieces by rude cast metal dies. They were then shaped with the mallet and hammer into the form required and put together. For other shapes the bodies were stamped in sections of three, four or six, and then put together. The art of shaping the metal into form by the spinning process was only partially known and only practised on a small scale. To have spun a teapot body

all in one piece would then have been considered a marvellous piece of work, and the head of the firm considered that when he could keep twenty makers-up going he would be satisfied.

"Of course, Mr Dixon soon found that his first estimate was far too modest; in 1823 he had 100 hands. . . . At the great exhibition of 1851 the firm received two prize medals and it was recorded that their exhibits of Britannia metal so closely resembled the sterling article that the authorities

Two candlesticks with (not visible) push-rod ejectors, of a type made in large quantities in the late 18th and 19th centuries, and a fiddle-pattern ladle.

recommended them to place over the case the words 'Britannia Metal Goods', lest they should be mistaken for silver.''

James Dixon and Sons also made silver and electroplated items. Dixon applied for a licence from Elkingtons to electroplate in 1848. This was comparatively late: other manufacturers who decided early to produce electroplate as well as Britannia metal were John Harrison and H. D. Wilkinson. By the mid-19th century the electroplating of Britannia metal was found to be possible. Shirley Bury, in *Victorian Electroplate* tells how the technique was discovered around 1846 by Elkingtons, who passed the knowledge to Dixons. The mark EPBM (electroplate on Britannia metal) was first stamped on wares in the 1850s. Other marks used usually include the maker's name and a catalogue or inventory number (which is often confused by the unwary for the date of manufacture).

The age-old method of casting pewter was practised by fewer and fewer people during the 19th century. Many items were made in both hard metal and in the old soft metals, for example tobacco boxes, funnels, pepperettes, inkstands, chamber pots and medical instruments. Pewter pub mugs and related items such as drainers and bottle

A tobacco jar and wine funnel.

driers were the largest "pocket of resistance" to the Britannia trade in England, whilst in America Britannia metal was used to the virtual exclusion of softer metal for most of the middle years of the 19th century. By reason of their intrinsic qualities, certain items belong to the traditions of earlier times even though they were introduced as late as the 1820s (some measures for example). These wares have been discussed earlier, in chapters related to their country of origin.

In England an enormous increase in the number of public houses, coinciding with the 1826 introduction of the Imperial standard, kept the pewter trade in business. After 1820 the traditional tulip and tapering cylindrical mugs maintained their popularity whilst new forms emerged – U-shaped, with "broken" handles, some with lid and chairback thumbpiece; tapering with angular or tubular loop handles; and concave-sided mugs; all these were made with a variety of moulded

Casters of the late 18th and early 19th centuries, mostly of "hard metal". The caster second from the right is an earlier Dutch example, c. 1740.

Right A "Welsh hat" chamber pot, made to fit a commode; c. 1800, 7½in high.

Below A money box engraved with initials and dated 1846, 3¼in, and a spice box with two compartments in foliage form, 4½in.

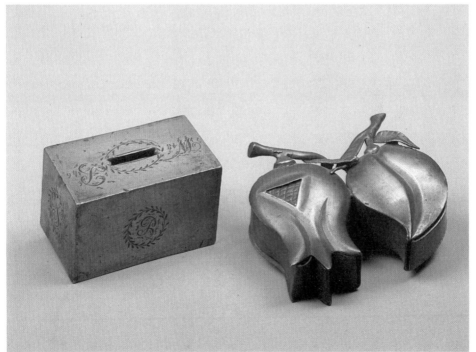

Above English pub mugs, mostly pint capacity. *Left to right* U-shaped, with double-scroll handle, by Sanders and Son, London (the wooden plug was used to straighten out dents in the body); cylindrical, with "attention" terminal to the handle, made in London c. 1810; barrel-shaped, by Samuel Cocks, c. 1830; quart capacity, tapering cylindrical, the scroll handle with heart-shaped terminal, c. 1800; rare baluster-shaped example by Llewellyn, Bristol, c. 1845–50.

Left A German spouted flagon (*Schnabelstitze*) dated 1861 and marked "Probzinn", 9in; a two-handled English mug, engraved after 1916, a popular form of sporting trophy made in the 19th century and often incorporating (like many pub mugs) a glass base; and a drainer from below a beer-barrel tap.

and reeded girdles and sometimes with glass bases. Some mugs were given side spouts for pouring into several smaller mugs or other drinking vessels. Many are engraved with owner's initials or with the name of the public house on either the body or underside. Bulbous lidless measures (also called "pot-belly" measures) were made in capacities from 1/32 pint to 1 gallon – a favourite item among collectors who seek to acquire the whole range. Although introduced right at the end of the 18th century, these lidless measures are basically a post-Imperial item.

Bulbous lidless "pot-belly" measures of gallon and quarter-gill capacities. Collectors often look for the whole range of sizes between; the smaller measures sometimes have brass rims.

Left English mugs: quart, cylindrical on tuck-in base with double-scroll handle; pint, tulip-shaped, with double-scroll handle; half-pint, cylindrical, with moulded girdles and handle with "attention" terminal; quart, U-shaped, with angular handle; half-pint, concave-sided; quart, U-shaped, with moulded bands, side spout and double-scroll handle.

Left, below English brass-rimmed tavern mugs of quart, pint and half-pint capacity.

Above A tapering octagonal and an ovoid coffee pot and a compressed spherical teapot, all of Britannia metal.

Teapots, coffee pots and milk jugs were mostly made in Britannia metal, keeping abreast of silver styles. Britannia metal pieces were the favourite presentation for sporting activities – homes were full of mugs and cups inscribed as rowing, tennis, cricket and archery trophies. Many medical instruments were made in pewter, including caster oil spoons, bleeding bowls, syringes and eye baths. Snuff boxes, too, were made in an infinite variety of styles. The simple rectangular or oval examples often had some scene – sporting, domestic, urban or rural – on the lid, surrounded by geometric or floral motifs. Others – "novelty" boxes – were made in the shape of a shoe, a pistol or a pin cushion, for example.

Elsewhere in Europe plates and food containers of all types were made in pewter well into the middle of the century. The traditional bowls and dishes – both for serving at table and for carrying food out-of-doors – were still used. Plainness and simplicity of design are paramount, although traces of the homely influence of the Biedermeier style of 1830–40 can sometimes be seen and the Empire style

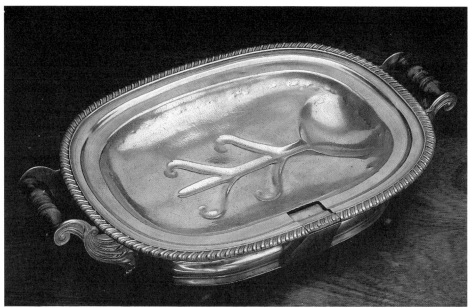

Below This hot water plate (made in the late 18th century by "J.I." of Bewdley, England) is a type that was particularly popular for much of the 19th century; 12¼in. The hot water was poured in through a hole in the small hinged section shown raised.

lingered in items such as coffee pots and milk jugs in France and Germany. Flagons and tankards sometimes have decorative schemes which reveal an attempt to introduce contemporary motifs, but on the whole, because of the restricted market for pewter at this time, there was no desire to keep abreast of the silver fashions such as there had been in the rococo and neo-classical periods. In a small way, however, mannerist and gothic revivals were recognized. For example reproductions of Briot's designs appear on a variety of

Left, above Four snuff boxes, late 18th to early 19th century.

Left A good example of a decorated meat dish with hot-water compartment underneath, gadrooned borders and turned wood handles. The average size of these dishes is 23–24in.

Right The top of a German barrel-shaped tankard, the lid centred with a medallion depicting imperial trophies and the lid border stamped with stiff leafage.

Left Two examples of German stitzen (both 13½in) illustrating how these developed from earlier forms (see pp. 100–102). The one on ball feet is inscribed and dated 1792. The other stitze, of hard metal, has a front recess with a figure of a landsknecht or knight beneath pseudo-armorials, on winged cherub-mask feet and with a dolphin finial; 2nd half 19th century.

Right A beaker bearing views of Hamburg; 4½in. This form of pictorial decoration, which developed in the 2nd half of the last century, is still popular in Germany today.

pieces. Detailed relief decoration was used to adorn tankards and beakers, in a fashion that is still popular today, particularly in Germany. Panoramic views surround the body of a piece – the sort of souvenir people liked to buy (and still do) to commemorate a visit. Figure finials and thumbpieces of exaggerated proportions depict men drinking or fighting.

In Scandinavia tankards continued to be made in 18th century style, though changes can be seen (p. 165). In France the Napoleonic unification of metric measures was important (see p. 80) and fewer measures were made in regional styles. Sometimes relief decoration such as fleur-de-lis, armorials, foliage or monsters, is seen on measures (particularly from Normandy). The 19th-century love of opulence and crowded decor often destroyed the classic simplicity of a piece. Heavily cast plates with wavy-edged rims were also made with this coarse relief decoration, making them suitable only for display purposes. At the turn of the century many of these pieces were made by A. Chaumette in Paris. The desire for flamboyance is seen in Germany, too. Stitzen continued to be made in fairly large quantities and the sturdy shapes of the 17th and 18th centuries became taller and more slender, with a pronounced flare at the base, which rested on three feet. These sometimes take the form of roundels, matching the ball thumbpiece, or are winged cherub's heads, similar to those found on 17th-century pewter. Many of these pieces are made of hard metal and lack the weight of earlier stitzen.

In general, the traditional styles of pewter measures, flagons and tankards continued to evolve as they had done in the past, but the once robust or graceful designs had become effete.

Marking in the 19th century became rather haphazard. The guilds had ceased to have control and by the end of the century connections between the makers and any surviving guilds or similar associations were very tenuous. Pewter measures used in pubs, taverns or other public places had the capacity mark (whether it be Imperial standard in England or metric as in France), and the maker's mark, usually stamped on the base or lip. In continental Europe the lip of a measure is often littered with the yearly stamps of inspectors. In England there is also the borough or county mark. The tradition of stamping the maker's touch inside the base of a piece or on the handle also continued on the continent. The marks placed on hard metal usually consisted of the full name of the maker stamped incuse and the serial number for the design. Occasionally the firm's trademark was also stamped, for example a trumpet and banner for James Dixon and Sons.

Top to bottom A "treasury" inkstand, with one side for pens, the other, divided in three, for ink, pounce and wafers; an inkwell with a porcelain well, a type once common in banks, post offices, and schools; a cylindrical well with side pen-rest.

This German dish is dated 1747 but was decorated considerably later with pseudoarmorials; 11¾in.

The rather sad tale of pewter during the 19th century has its foundations in the 18th century. Throughout Europe and America pewter's popularity steadily declined as it lost favour to pottery and glass as the materials most commonly used for household utensils. The process of changing over was relatively slow but is now complete, and it is difficult for us to realize today just how important a part pewter used to play in the life of a household. Present-day comparisons may well be the use of plastics and man-made fibres in place of natural materials such as paper, wood, wool and cotton.

No clearer evidence of the reduction of a once powerful trade can be found than that of the sale catalogues of moulds and tools sold by Englefields of London in 1888–9. Similar sales were most probably held by many other firms throughout Europe. The history of Englefields also shows how the tools, traditional skills and goodwill of a business sometimes pass through many hands. In 1700 Thomas Scattergood was elected Freeman of the Pewterers' Company. His business was continued in 1716 by Edward Meriefield, who in turn was succeeded by John Townsend in 1748. In 1785 Thomas Compton joined his father-in-law John Townsend to form the partnership Townsend and Compton. After several partnerships within the Compton family, the firm was absorbed into that of Elmslie and Simpson in 1868, to become Brown and Englefield in 1885 when, under James Englefield, it was the only surviving firm of pewterers in London. The firm still produces high-quality cast pewter.

ART NOUVEAU TO CONTEMPORARY

When in 1875 Arthur Lasenby Liberty (1843–1917) opened his shop in London, it was filled with oriental materials – a stock which soon included porcelain as well. Like many of his contemporaries, he was influenced by the displays of Japanese wares at the International Exhibition in 1862 which gave rise to the Aesthetic Movement – a fashion for things Japanese which extended to materials, porcelain, furniture and furnishings, silver and metalwork, though not to pewter. During the years of the popularity of the Aesthetic Movement, 1865–90, people became increasingly concerned about the dominance of machine-made mass-produced goods which were poorly designed and made. They rejected many of the ideals of the Great Exhibition of 1851. There was a desire to return to craftsmanship and quality, ambitions which did not necessarily mean forsaking commercialism and modern techniques.

Early in the 1880s these ideals found expression in a new style. It emerged in France, Belgium and England, but the name by which it came to be known was taken from that chosen by Samuel Bing in 1895 for his shop in Paris – L'Art Nouveau. The influence of this new movement spread throughout Europe, reaching the height of its popularity around 1900. In Germany the style was known as "Jugendstil" after the magazine *Jugend* founded in 1896, in Austria it was called "Sezessionstil".

For the first time since the Renaissance the arts were seen as a single movement; designers aimed to create buildings and their interiors which blended and were the result of one theme, not a muddle of disparate ideas thrown together. Interior decoration especially gained respectability as an art form. Architecture and the design of furniture and objects, whether they be made in porcelain, glass, metal or on paper, were practised by the same people – and pewter was brought out of hibernation to play its part.

The feeling most clearly expressed by Art Nouveau is movement. The swirling lines curl and twist, sometimes with wonderful simplicity, sometimes in interlaced patterns of great complexity. In this linear movement the forms of nature play an important part and so too does the female figure – rising out of the folds of a vase or bowl, adorning the side of a mirror or inkstand. Within the style national characteristics emerge in pewter. Much of the German work is sharp, the thin lines carried at times to extraordinary shapes – made possible by the high antimony content in their pewter. In contrast other designers in Germany and Austria worked in soft moulded shapes reminiscent of the 17th-century auricular or of the 18th-century rococo styles. In France the use of flowers and foliage and the modelling of the female face were dominant. This naturalistic element was important in England too, where objects were more

A vase, c. 1900, by WMF; 8¾in.

A claret jug, c. 1900, of pewter and green glass by WMF; 8¼in.

compact, less extravagant than on the continent. The Art Nouveau style was developed far more successfully in the decorative arts than in painting, Because of the emphasis placed on equality of materials used, pewter was drawn into this flow of ideas alongside silver, bronze and jewellery, and objects were actually designed to be made in pewter rather than the pewterer either reproducing the traditional shapes of his predecessors or slavishly copying designs intended for other metals (as had happened ever since the era of *Edelzinn*). But of course the majority of these pieces were not made by a craftsman pewterer – they were made by large workshops (the biggest were metalwork factories) who made objects in pewter as well as in silver, bronze and other base metals.

Germany produced the largest quantity of pewter in the late 19th and early 20th centuries and exported on a big scale. The largest factory was Württembergische Metall-warenfabrik, or WMF, who manufactured electroplated wares as well as pewter. WMF was founded in 1853 by Daniel Straub and greatly expanded under Carl Haegel from 1880–1900 after the Straub family firm's amalgamation with A. Ritter & Co. in 1880. WMF aimed at the mass market, producing a wide range of table garnitures, vases, bowls, trays, inkstands, tea and coffee sets. Many of their designs are characterized by the use of the female figure – as the centre for a dessert dish or lying beside the pen tray of an

A table centrepiece, c. 1900, by WMF; 10½in high.

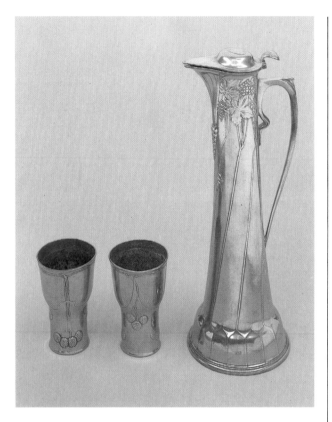

A claret jug and goblets, marked "Osiris", made c. 1900 by Walter Scherf & Co., Nuremberg; 13½ and 4½in.

inkstand, the the folds of her clothing merging into and forming the bowl or tray which she adorns. The jugs and bowls frequently have streamlined, thin handles. These contrast with the softer, more gently moulded forms seen in bowls and vases made by another major producer of pewter, J. P. Kayser and Son, who from 1874 used the trade name Kayserzinn. The firm was headed by Engelbert Kayser and had its design offices in Cologne, although the factory was near Krefeld. They exhibited a lot of pewter at the Paris Exhibition of 1900. Hugo Leven (b. 1874) designed some of their best pieces. Among other manufacturers were Ferdinand Hubert Schmitz of Rheinische Bronzegiesserei, who produced "Orivit" pewter from 1901 at Köln-Ehrenfeld; Walter Scherf & Co. in Nuremberg, whose work is often marked "Osiris"; and Metallwaren-Fabrik Eduard Hueck of Lüdenshied, founded in 1864. Some of their work was designed by Peter Behrens and Albin Müller, and also by Josef Maria Olbrich. Olbrich's monogram, J. O. in a square, is sometimes seen on his pieces as a designer's mark. He was a

A tray (23½in) and cake basket (13¼in) c. 1901, both marked "Orivit", made by Hubert Schmitz, Köln-Ehrenfeld.

A tea service designed by Hugo Leven (1874–1956), and made c. 1900 by J. P. Kayser and Son, Krefeld; marked "Kayserzinn".

founder member of the Vienna Secession in 1897. Another firm, F. & M. (Felsenstein und Mainzer) in Nuremberg, marked their work "Norica Zinn". "Bingit Zinn" pewterware was produced by Nürnberger Metall-und-Lackierwaren Fabrik, founded in 1895 by the Bing brothers; "Orion" pewter was also made in Nuremberg in the 1890s. In Munich, Ludwig Mory's firm was founded in 1883. The Germans and Austrians were enormously influenced by the great Belgian designer Henri van de Velde (1863–1957) who was a pioneer of Art Nouveau and moved to Germany.

J. P. Kayser and Son, Walter Scherf & Co. and L. Lichtinger of Munich (among whose designers in the 1890s was Karl Gross) were among the firms who from 1899 exported pewter to Liberty's in London. In that year Liberty began to sell silver under the "Cymric" label and he followed this in 1903 with the "Tudric" range of pewter. Most of the silver and all the pewter was made for him by the Birmingham firm W. H. Haseler. (Haseler also made some pewter marked

A coffee pot, c. 1910, designed by Peter Behrens and made by Eduard Hueck; 9in.

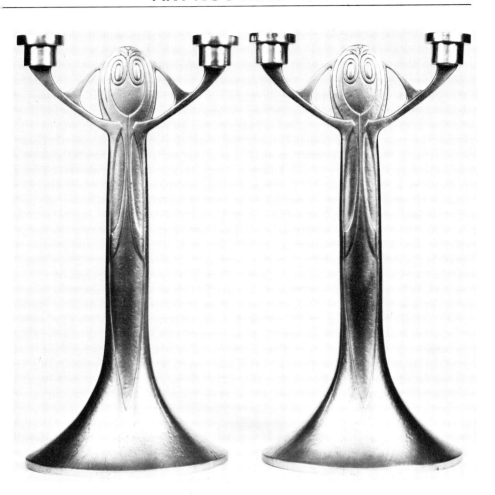

Above A pair of candelabra marked "Silberzinn E. Hueck", designed by Josef Olbrich, with characteristic Viennese linear motifs; 14½in.

Right A rose bowl, designed by Rex Silver for the Liberty "Tudric" range; c. 1903, 5¾in.

Left A clock, with enamelled face, designed by Archibald Knox for Liberty and Co.; c. 1905, 8¾in.

Above A plate and a teapot made by Kayser, c. 1900.

"Solkets".) Liberty adopted for his designs "the motif and lines of ancient celtic ornament. . . supplemented by floral and plant motifs". His products were as closely related to, and influenced by, the British Arts and Crafts movement led by Charles Robert Ashbee's Guild of Handicraft (founded in 1888), as to the extravagant flowing lines of Art Nouveau. Liberty's principal metalwork designer was Archibald Knox, who joined Liberty in 1901. Knox, a friend of the influential designer Christopher Dresser, studied celtic design in the Isle of Man and his work in pewter typifies his style of interlaced strapwork with stylized flowers, angular or crescent-shaped handles and the use of blue-green enamels. He was joined by Reginald ("Rex") Silver. Their prolific output included bowls, mirrors, clocks, vases, boxes, jugs and teasets.

Another designer in England who worked in pewter as well as silver (though not for Liberty) was Gilbert Marks. He worked in Croydon, Surrey, from about 1885. The Century Guild, established in 1882 as part of the craft movement, also produced pewter wares.

In France Jules Brateau exhibited pewter in the 1900 Paris Exhibition. The medallist Alexandre Charpentier and Jules Desbois designed pewter as did Antoine Pompe in Belgium. Decorative pewter made in the Netherlands from 1900 is often marked "Urania". In Scandinavia, Denmark and Sweden were the centres of design throughout this period. Mogens Ballin (1871–1914) and other designers such as Siegfried Wagner, J. F. Willumsen, Gudmund Hentze and Ludvig Find, worked in pewter at the turn of the century. Georg Jensen (1866–1935) stands out among designers and manufacturers for his continuing success. Although he worked in silver, Jensen's clear, simple lines were in the forefront of all Scandinavian design and have had a lasting influence. The work of his firm in pewter is discussed towards the end of this chapter.

The quality of metal used everywhere was of a high standard. Liberty and the continental makers who were several years ahead of him in the manufacture of metalwork, realized that modern demands were different from those of the days when pewter enjoyed its greatest popularity and played an important utilitarian part in every household. Its use at the very end of the 19th century was bound to be different. In 1904 Liberty read a paper "Pewter and the revival of its uses" to the Society of Arts and even though the objects he produced in the Tudric range differed widely stylistically from the pieces he had imported earlier from Germany, the sentiments he expressed (allowing for different

A covered bowl, c. 1905 marked "Solkets"; the design, which is attributed to Archibald Knox, has typical entwined strap work; 5½in.

A late (c. 1920) example of Liberty pewter, this teaset has a hammered finish and heat-resistant wicker-covered handles.

interpretation and taste) explain the thoughts behind the revival of pewter at this time. "The ideal of modern English pewter. . . aims at more than a commercial success – it aims at a high standard in design, a high standard in workmanship, and a high standard in the quality of the metal and it strives to avoid over-modelling and over-chasing. It would devote attention to shapes being properly adapted to the several purposes for which the objects are made, it would see that the constructive lines be graceful, well contrasted and strong, and that ornament, when used at all, be used with restraint and grow out of the general design. These excellent intentions, unfortunately, are not always carried out, for faulty and eccentric moves strike out from time to time." (*Journal of the Society of Arts*, May 17, 1904).

Art Nouveau was short-lived – some people still dismiss it as a fashionable craze. The movement as a whole was most popular in the years 1895–1905. It is perhaps unfortunate that during the time most of the pewter was made (1900–1914) many designers were already turning away from the style and seeking fresh ideas.

Among these was Josef Hoffmann in Vienna. In 1903, together with Koloman Moser, he founded the Wiener Werkstatte and began to develop a new style in which geometry succeeded the curves of Art Nouveau. In Holland, towards the end of the First World War the "de Stijl" designers based their name on a magazine edited by Theo van Doesburg. In America pewter was designed, among others, by Josef Hoffmann's son and daughter-in-law Pola and Wolfgang Hoffmann for the Early American Pewter

ART NOUVEAU TO CONTEMPORARY

Company, and by Gilbert Rohde for Wilcox. Liberty's continued to make pewter until 1938, producing, among other items, tea and coffee sets with a deliberately hammered finish. Most of the moulds were melted to help the war effort in 1939–45.

Several designers and crafstmen whose work was first noticed in the inter-war period of the 1920s and 1930s are still influential today, particularly in Scandinavia. The firm of Georg Jensen, mentioned earlier, remains a leader, selling pewter designed for them by Just Andersen (1884–1943) and Astrid Fog. Andersen was influenced by the work of Mogens Ballin. His work includes a wide range of domestic wares – tea and coffee sets, plates, cruets, serving dishes, beakers, vases and candlesticks. Andersen's business was bought by A. Michelson, which in turn was acquired by Royal Copenhagen Porcelain. Royal Copenhagen Porcelain also recently bought Georg Jensen, so that the work of both Andersen and Jensen is now under the same "umbrella". Jensen's leading designer today is Henning Koppel, who has recently begun to design in pewter as well as silver, continuing to create pieces in which form and clarity of line are of the utmost importance.

Whilst in Denmark Jensen and Andersen created designs which stood apart from the work of their contemporaries elsewhere, in Sweden the work of Estrid Erikson in the late

A plate by Just Andersen (8½in) and a bowl and two candlesticks by Astrid Fog.

Above right A candelabrum and vase by Just Andersen; 7¼ and 10¼in.

Right A plate, mug and covered bowl by Henning Koppel for Georg Jensen; 8¾, 2¾ and 2¾in.

ART NOUVEAU TO CONTEMPORARY

Left An "Art Deco" tea set by Gilbert Rohde for Wilcox, incorporating bakelite handles; 1929.

Right A vase by Henning Koppel for Georg Jensen.

1920s and early 1930s covered an enormous range showing also the importance of Scandinavian design. Estrid Erikson started the firm Svenskt Tenn in 1924. It soon developed into a leading interior decorating business employing designers such as Josef Frank (1885–1967), whose association with the firm began in 1932. Svenskt Tenn's catalogue of 1931, for example, includes a few bowls, candlesticks and beakers in "traditional" pewter designs, but also contains tables, hand-mirrors, dressing-table mirrors, sconces, table lamps, boxes and inkstands using motifs and designs which today would be called "Odeon style" or "Art Deco". However, such labels must always be used very cautiously, particularly when describing the early works of living artists. Estrid Erikson continues to design pewter today, some of which is illustrated.

The importance of form was stressed by one of America's

Salad servers by Shirley Charron.

leading pewterers, Frances Felten, who died in 1976. She wrote in Shirley Charron's book *Modern Pewter, Design and Techniques*: "Pewter is best left to depend on form and line for its beauty, as most types of surface enrichment are out of place with the simple, rather robust contours that this ware calls for. . . . The effects of light, shadow and texture are just as important as those of line and form." This, surely, expresses the thoughts of pewterers since the Middle Ages. Frances Felten was in the forefront of the revival of interest in pewter and crafts generally in America in the post-war years, passing on her skills to many students. Her work is formed by hand, soldered together or beaten, from sheet pewter. It includes candlesticks, coffee services, pitchers, mugs, ice buckets, cocktail shakers, bowls and a range of boxes, many of which incorporate enamels by Margaret Seeler, or knops and handles in rosewood. The majority of pewterers in America today come from New England, principally Connecticut, most of them working in pewter as a part-time occupation.

In complete contrast to the polished work of these designers is that of Hein Molenaar, whose work has a matt finish. After apprenticeship in Germany, Hein Molenaar

Jug and two beakers by Alain Henry, Vendôme, France.

worked in Holland and France, where he now lives. He uses almost no machinery, hand-raising objects from sheets cut to shape, either by hammering or hand-folding. Each piece is original — only very rarely will he repeat a design on special request — and his work shows total individuality of design.

In Germany the work of Volkhard Bläse is also hammered, with a textured surface. Among other leading makers are Albrecht Röders and the firm of Ludwig Mory in Munich (mentioned earlier). Pewterers in Germany today are concentrated in Bavaria and Baden-Württemberg.

The revival of interest in crafts and traditional ideas in the late 19th century saved pewter from total extinction but modern manufacturing techniques were used. Some of the largest firms of today were founded at the end of the 19th century during the pewter revival, for example J. N. Daalderop, the makers of "Royal Holland Pewter" in Tiel, who were founded in 1880. Others, such as PMC (Sheffield) Ltd, have been founded within the last 15 years. Whilst many firms today produce pewter to contemporary designs, a large

Above A jug by Hein Molenaar.

Right A tea caddy or tobacco jar by Svenskt Tenn, designed by Estrid Erikson.

proportion of their work is to make "traditional" pewter to satisfy the demands of the mass market who think that this is what pewter *should* look like. Pewter is thus typecast in most people's minds – as it has been for many hundreds of years. And so the larger manufacturers produce pieces which either update earlier domestic styles (for example "Stuart" style) or are reproductions of traditional pewter. These latter pieces fall into two categories: the first is direct reproduction, quite often using old moulds; the second includes those pieces which reproduce an earlier Rembrandt-kan, guild flagon or kelchkanne, for example, but which are historically inaccurate in some way – the angle of the body, thickness of handle or shape of thumbpiece. A measure is sometimes made in a size never found in earlier times or it is spun when previously it would have been cast. Old moulds are ingeniously re-used to produce different items, for example the base and lower part of the body of a baluster mug is made into an ashtray or small bowl. Modern lead-free pewter, even those pieces given the "antique" finish, does not, in any case, look old and may never achieve the patina of older pieces. These are quite distinct from fakes – those items made deliberately to deceive the purchaser.

Although this type of work may be produced today in greater quantity, the importance of contemporary design and the continual growth of craftsmanship and individualism

A tea and coffee set by Harald Buchrucker of Ludwigsburg.

cannot be over-emphasized. It is vital that people continue to commission work and encourage the craft of the pewterer. Pewter today fights competition from stainless steel (which is cheap and very amenable to contemporary design) and from silver plate (which, in spite of poor design and workmanship, is often mistakenly thought to be "better" than pewter). Although motivated by very different ideals, the two techniques – mass-production and individual hand-crafting – must develop together as they always have done, good design and workmanship being the criteria of success.

A tankard of cast pewter by Ludwig Mory of Munich.

PEWTER MARKS

When the craftsman was accepted into his guild the new pewter master's marks were punched into the guild's touchplate or register of masters. This 17th-century touchplate from Lille in north-west France illustrates the hammer/crown/maker's initials combination, the rose and crown quality mark, and the use of the town device (in the case of Lille, a fleur-de-lys).

In the small space available it is impossible to give a comprehensive selection of marks. However, it is hoped that those shown, together with the few examples listed under the various types of marks, will help to guide the reader to discover the area in which a piece was made. For more precise information – to check on the master, his dates and his town – it will be necessary to turn to other books. The bibliography indicates those books which are the most useful for tracing marks; many of these are the result of deep and lengthy research by their authors. Some of the other books listed also have a selection of marks.

Marks were usually stamped on a piece when it was completed, but sometimes a mark was incorporated into the mould and therefore cast into the piece (see illustration on p. 236). Many pieces bear no marks. This may be because a piece is early, made before marking was regularly practised, or because it was made by a travelling pewterer, or perhaps to avoid penalization by pewter guild or company searchers if poor quality metal was deliberately used.

Touch marks, or "touches" serve two fundamental purposes: to identify the maker and his native town, and to show the quality of the metal. Craftsmen began to mark their pewter in the early Middle Ages to guarantee the quality of their work and possibly to avoid being wrongly held responsible for the poor quality of another's product. The practice of marking pewter grew throughout the 14th century: for example in 1382 pewterers in Paris were forbidden to sell hammered work without first marking it (probably the origin of the hammer mark in France). However it was not general practice to mark until the 16th century.

The methods of marking were governed by law and by decrees issued by the guilds. The administration of the marking system was one of the prime occupations of the guilds and, generally speaking, they were able to maintain fairly strict authority over their members, although frequent abuses with regard to marking and quality are reported in guild records.

Over the years both the style and content of marks altered. Until the mid-17th century most marks were quite small. Thereafter, in the late 17th and 18th centuries, marks became larger (some approximately 1in wide) although small marks continued to be used as well. Fashion dictated the shape of a cartouche, whether circular or quatrefoil, architectural, within crossed palm fronds, assymetrical, or in the form of a neo-classical shield. In the 19th century many marks were simply plain rectangles. In Britannia metal some marks were stamped incuse (see p. 233).

The text which follows groups marks according to the information they give. Only a few examples are given in each case and the selection is not definitive.

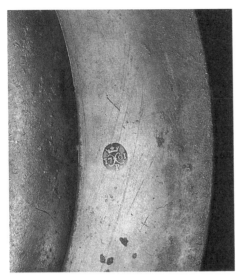

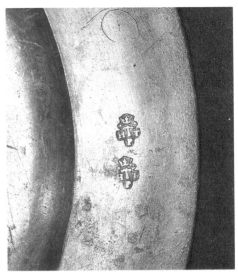

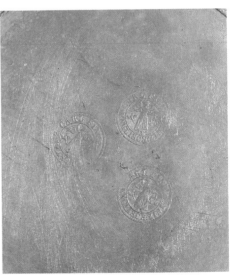

Top left France. Town ("P" for Paris), fine quality (double scrolling "F") and date (first use of the punch) marks.

Top right France. A shaped punch of the 17th and early 18th centuries, this one with the maker's initials (HT), the usual hammer and crown mark, and "P" for Paris.

Below left A German maker's touch on the handle of a 17th-century guild flagon, showing on the dexter of the shield the eagle of Nuremberg and on the sinister the maker's initials.

(Taken from the flagon shown on p. 21).

Below right An 18th-century German mark struck three times showing the master (Carl Finck) and quality (winged angels with scales above "Englisch Zinn").

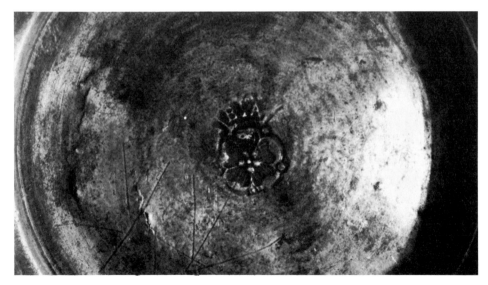

Top left Switzerland. A touch typical of the 17th and 18th centuries, showing the maker's initials of Bernhardt Wick and emblem of Basle. (From the stitze shown on p. 124.)

Top right 19th century, English. The outer numerals are the manufacturer's design number, the oval mark incorporates the maker's name and town and the diamond mark of the patent office. This PODR mark is commonly seen on 19th-century objects in a variety of materials.

Below Low Countries. These marks from the base of an 18th-century measure show the rose and crown quality mark incorporating the maker's initials in the crown (a characteristic of Low Countries pewter).

233

PEWTER MARKS

MAKER'S MARK

The maker's touch showed that he acknowledged responsibility for his work and in theory guaranteed its quality. It was usually in the form of a cartouche bearing his initials and possibly a device and sometimes the date of his entry into the guild. By the late 17th century the full name of the maker was frequently included in his touch and this was often combined with town and quality marks.

In France the outline of the early touch is either roughly an angular quatrefoil or a circle containing maker's initials, hammer and crown (mentioned earlier) and date. In the Low Countries the master's initials were incorporated into town or quality marks. In England the master's initials were combined with a pictorial symbol of his choice, possibly a punning pictorial reference to his name (for example, PC and a cart for Peter Carter, RC with a lamb holding a shepherd's crook for Robert Crooke, or TF and a fountain for Thomas Fountain). America copied the English style until the revolution, after which many marks included the eagle or liberty cap.

The size of workshops varied enormously. Sometimes a pewterer worked on his own or with a couple of assistants. However, some workshops employed a large staff and produced enormous quantities of pewter. It would have been impossible for Samuel Duncombe in Birmingham to make every dish and plate that bears his touch or for Thomas D. Boardman in America to have a hand in the making of every item produced in his works. Their marks showed that they were responsible for the manufacture of the piece, not that they actually made it. Today, firms such as Englefields in London or Georg Jensen in Copenhagen acknowledge this by stamping the mark of the craftsman or designer as well as that of the company (see p. 237).

TOWN MARK

The town mark takes several forms: the coat-of-arms, device or seal of the city or town; the name of the town in full; or an initial representing the full name.

Germany, France, Switzerland, Austria–Hungary and the Low Countries often used armorial bearings until the 17th century. Thereafter, as marks were amalgamated, the use was less widespread although it did continue. In England the stamping of a "London" label came into use in the 17th century but was soon being used by provincial pewterers too, for example those in Bristol and Birmingham. Thus the "London" label is no guarantee of provenance. Other examples of the use of a separate punch giving the full name of the city are Rotterdam and Stockholm. In America the town mark was either incorporated into the maker's mark or stamped separately. France used a system of initials from

British Isles

Thomas Alderson, London,
c. 1790–1825

Joseph Austen and Son, Cork, early
19th century

Allen Bright, Bristol, 18th century

Thomas Burford and James Green,
London, c. 1750–80

Robert Bush and Richard Perkins,
Bristol, c. 1800

Charles Clark, Waterford, c. 1790–1810

Alexander Cleeve, London, 18th century

Thomas Compton, London, early 19th century

Benjamin Cooper, London (master 1680)

John Carruthers Crane, Bewdley, early 19th century

John Duncombe, Birmingham, 18th century

the late 17th century (P=Paris, R=Rouen); this method was also practised elsewhere (W=Wien, Vienna).

Town marks and maker's marks were sometimes struck in specific combinations which can indicate provenance; in Switzerland two small shields were stamped very close, sometimes linked above by the initials of the maker.

In some places the town mark became obsolete in the 18th century when the provenance was included in the same mark as quality and maker.

QUALITY MARKS

Rose and Crown. Taken from the English Tudor rose and first used in England in the 16th century on goods to be exported, this mark soon spread to the continent, where it was used on items made from English tin and then as a mark of good quality. Fresh legislation had to be introduced when a previous rule had been consistently abused. The following extract from Dr J. van Deun, writing on "The pewterer's craft in Antwerp", describes one such alteration: "In 1535 permission was granted to employ the rosemark in view of the competition with the fine English pewter marked with the Tudor rose. However, the rose had to be accompanied by a master's mark. An ordinance of 1543 made the use of the rose mark obligatory. The same ordinance concerns the prevention of abuses in the entry into the guild. Illicit production and trade of pewter in the city as well as in the surrounding villages were undermining the standards of quality and threatened to give the pewter from Antwerp a bad name.... The ordinance of 3 February 1603 is a particularly important document. It concerns the competition with English pewter and regulates a long-standing although illicit custom of mixing fine English tin with material of a lower quality, so that the rose mark lost its value as a symbol of quality. Only the flat objects were to be made of pure English tin: the hard English variety was not suitable for smaller pieces, so that these less pure objects were given a new mark: a smaller English rose with the hand of Antwerp in its heart. From 1603 onwards all pewter had to carry a master's mark." (Exhibition catalogue, *Keur van Tin uit de Havensteden Amsterdam, Antwerpen en Rotterdam*, 1979.)

In England the rose and crown design was widely used as a mark of quality, especially on plates and dishes; marking was controlled by the Company. Design of the mark varied and it came to incorporate a variety of information: in England it frequently included plumage and the word London; in the Low Countries the maker's initials are included in the crown, either in the arch or on the circlet, and the rose sometimes has shading lines on the petals.

The rose and crown mark is also found in Germany, Austria, Hungary, Scandinavia, America and France (above

Top left British Isles. Crowned-X quality mark, maker's touch, "London" mark, and "hallmarks", typical of late 18th-/early 19th-century marks. (Base of the hot-water plate, p. 205.)

Top right British Isles. Date and maker's mark of William Scott of Edinburgh. The placing of this mark on the inside of the lid, and the fact that it is cast, it is unusual in British pewter.

Bottom left United States. Uncrowned "X", and maker's and town marks in simple rectangular punches. (From the 19th-century pitcher p. 183.)

Bottom right United States. Maker's mark of David Melville (1755–93) of Newport, Rhode Island, incorporating (and therefore post-1788) the liberty

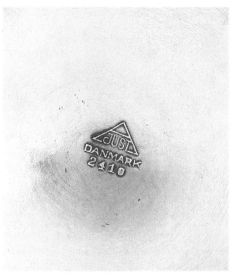

cap and stars of the twelve states, with "hallmarks".

Top left A contemporary maker's mark stamped incuse showing the name of the maker, the initials of the designer (Henning Koppel) and the design number.

Top right A contemporary maker's mark cast into a piece, showing maker (Just Andersen of Denmark), and design number. (Taken from the base of the vase on p. 223.)

Below Engraving on an 18th-century German plate showing a typical merchant's mark. Variations of this type of identifying mark were incorporated into maker's touches and also in seals (for example signet rings and branding irons) to denote ownership. (See p. 243.)

PEWTER MARKS

all in the north east area, e.g. Valenciennes, Lille).

Angel. A mark to show good quality pewter – the figure of a winged angel sometimes representing Justice holding scales and palm. This mark was not used in England or America but was in widespread use from the 18th century onwards in the Low Countries (often incorporated into "hall-marks"), Germany, Austria, Scandinavia, Hungary, the eastern border of France (e.g. Mulhouse, Strasbourg), Switzerland and elsewhere. This mark, particularly in Austria and Germany, came to incorporate all necessary information, i.e. maker, town, date, and frequently also the words "Engelzinn", "Feinzinn" etc.

X, sometimes crowned. Stamped separately, sometimes incuse. This mark was used (and mis-used) in England on flatware from the late 17th century to indicate pewter of "extraordinary" quality or "hard metal", probably containing a minimal quantity of lead and a small percentage of antimony. At a slightly later date in Germany (Thuringia and Saxony) it may indicate an alloy of 10 : 1 tin to lead. The mark is also found in the Low Countries and America.

Examples of its use on pieces other than flatware are on "haystack" measures made by Joseph Austen & Son of Cork, or Victorian pub mugs (by which time it had ceased to have its original meaning).

Letter and coats-of-arms. In Switzerland pewter containing 10% or less lead was stamped with an "F" crowned. In France from 1676 fine pewter was marked with a double F crowned, whilst ordinary pewter was marked with a C crowned (for "common" quality).

In Sweden from 1754 the heraldic shield bearing three crowns on an azure field (indicated by horizontal lines) was used on high quality items.

Words. In the 18th century composition of the metal was denoted by a variety of words, sometimes included in the angel or rose marks. This practice was most common in Germany, Austria, Hungary, France and Switzerland. Regulations varied from region to region and "Feinzinn" (for example) was used to describe pure tin or that of the finest quality in one region and ordinary quality pewter in another.

The following are a few of the many labels used: Feinzinn; Probzinn; Alte Probe, to indicate that the piece has been re-cast from an old alloy; Blockzinn, Blocktin; Kronzinn, usually a ratio of 15:1 or 12:1; Schlechteszinn, poor quality; Englisch (or Engels) Zin(n), metal purified to English standards or using English tin; Etain fin, Estain, Estin, used in France and Switzerland to show less than 10% lead; Sonnant, also less than 10% lead; Etain commun, ordinary pewter.

In England the most popular label was "superfine hard metal".

Samuel Duncombe, Birmingham, 18th century

John Gardner, Edinburgh, 18th century

Richard Going, Bristol, 18th century

Graham and Wardrop, Glasgow, late 18th–early 19th century

Thomas Haward, London, 2nd half 17th century

238

Thomas Inglis, Edinburgh, early 18th century

Edward Leapidge, London, 18th century

Robert Sadler, Newcastle, 18th century

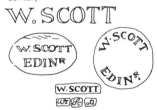

William Scott, Edinburgh, late 18th–early 19th century

Samuel Smith, London (master 1727)

Bodenrosette. In Switzerland, Austria, Hungary, Germany and eastern France, the base of hollow-ware is often centred by a cast rosette. The design varies and sometimes includes the initials of the maker. Some marks show other devices, such as a bear rampant in Switzerland.

"HALLMARKS"

A series of three or four small marks placed close together resembling silver hallmarks. These marks were struck by pewterers in England from the early 17th century, deliberately copying the marks used on silver – presumably in an attempt to upgrade their wares in the eyes of the customer. From 1635 onwards the Goldsmiths' Company made repeated protests to the Pewterers' Company, who were quite unable to prevent the practice (which was entirely unauthorized). The series of marks usually contains the maker's initials together with one or more of the following: lion passant, leopard's head, Britannia, lion rampant, harp, thistle, buckle, or anchor.

The use spread to the continent, particularly to northwest Germany and the Low Countries, where the series frequently included a flying angel mark and town arms. Marks on Swedish pewter also simulate hallmarks.

DATE

The date included in the touchmark in many countries either indicates the date of the legislation under which the piece was marked or records the master's entry into a guild. Sometimes, however, succeeding generations of a family continued to use the earlier dates of their ancestor's admission, as if to say "established since. . ."

The date does not show the year in which the piece was made and pewter generally does not bear date letters in the same way as silver. The exception is Sweden, where date letters were stamped from 1694. The system was regularized in 1759 to bring pewter into line with silver marking and this practice continued unbroken until 1912.

Numbers stamped in the late 19th and the 20th century are design numbers and do not show the date of manufacture.

CAPACITY AND VERIFICATION MARKS

In several countries hollow-ware which was used to serve drink in public was tested for capacity. This was usually done when the piece was first made but some areas were subject to annual inspection. These marks are quite separate from the words often stamped on the front of a piece to indicate capacity (pint, quart, litre, demi-litre).

In *Les Étains*, M. Boucaud and M. Frégnac illustrate (plate 221) a 17th-century measure from the Low Countries, its lip

239

PEWTER MARKS

covered in capacity stamps, and (plate 184) a Cologne measure of the 18th century with similar stamps on the lid. In France and the Low Countries metric measures were stamped at the lip each year on inspection with small punches using sequential letters, France using the Roman alphabet with Flemish measures showing the Greek alphabet (see illustration p. 151).

In England Acts of Parliament standardized capacities for ale and wine measures. Seals of verification most commonly seen are those relating to Acts passed in the reigns of William III (1688) and Queen Anne (1704 and 1707). Pieces with earlier seals are exceedingly rare. The seal of verification used in Queen Anne's reign was AR below a crown. That of William III (WR below a crown) was used during his reign and again, after Queen Anne's death in 1714, right through the 18th century until 1826. When Imperial Standard came into force in that year, the marks changed to GIV then WIV, and VR, sometimes with the word "Imperial" or with heraldic borough and county stamps (denoted by numbers after 1879). Many of these are listed by C. A. Peal in *British Pewter*.

THE PLACING OF MARKS
The placing of marks can give an indication of date, quality and area of manufacture. A few examples are given.

Area of manufacture and date. In England early 17th-century flagons are sometimes marked half-way down the handleback but it would be rare to find an English flagon, tankard or mug of any date marked on the handle just below the hinge — a favourite spot for marks in Switzerland, Germany and Austria–Hungary, for example.

The marking of hollow-ware on the outside of the lid is universal. In England it is restricted to the 17th century and early years of the 18th century (see p. 36) and in the British Isles it is unusual to find marks inside the lid (which is common on 18th-century Germany tankards, for example), except on some measures from Scotland (for example those by William Scott of Edinburgh) and the Channel Islands (notably IDSX for John de St Croix).

English and American hollow-ware is often marked on the body near the handle (see p. 57), a practice which is rarely found on the continent except for capacity and control marks.

The marking of flatware was fairly universal: until the first two decades of the 18th century hallmarks are usually found on the front of the rim. At the end of the 17th century the practice of placing marks on the underside began and this continued until the 19th century. Marks were stamped either on the reverse of the rim or in the centre of the plate or dish.

Joseph Spackman, London, 18th century

Townsend and Compton, London, early 19th century

James Yates, Birmingham, early 19th century

Yates, Birch and Spooner, Birmingham, c. 1800

unknown maker, T.B., c. 1680

unknown maker, H.F., c. 1680 (touchmark and "hallmarks")

unknown maker, I.G., c. 1700

verification stamp relating to Act of William III, used between 1680 and 1826

verification stamp, reign of George IV (1820–30) and Imperial Standard mark (from 1826)

John de St Croix, Jersey, 18th century

Hellier Perchard of Guernsey (worked in London), 18th century

France

Paris town and quality marks, 1701 and 1719

Quality was sometimes indicated by the way marks were struck. For example in Sweden there were three approved standards of pewter. Black metal (66% tin) was struck with two identical maker's marks; common pewter (83% tin) bore one town mark as well as the two maker's marks; and fine pewter (97% tin) was struck four times, twice with the maker's mark and twice with the town mark. Elsewhere, a mark struck twice usually indicates high quality, but sometimes the repeated striking of a touch has apparently no significance other than the whim of the pewterer (as in England).

FAKES

It is possible only to give a few examples. If a reproduction piece has been cast by making a mould from an earlier item, the resulting piece will bear the marks cast into it. These usually lack the crispness of properly stamped marks. Often a modern piece of pewter is struck with the wrong type of mark (e.g. Samuel Duncombe marks on a tappit-hen). Sometimes a reproduction piece bears the right type of mark, which is known to be a false punch, through previously discovered examples.

Some reference books now include a section on known fake marks (e.g. *Les Étains* by M. Boucaud and M. Frégnac, and *More Pewter Marks* by C. A. Peal).

OWNERSHIP

Marks of ownership have no connection with touchmarks but sometimes cause doubt. They fall into three categories: engraved armorials, showing either the full coat-of-arms or the crest or badge of the family (pp. 48–9); stamped house-mark (see p. 114); or initials, either punched or engraved, either in a row (see p. 153) or in a triad (these are sometimes crowned, but this does not indicate that the owners are titled) – e.g. $_W^PV$ – William and Vanessa Parker. The style of engraving, particularly of initials, is often a useful guide to provenance.

241

PEWTER MARKS

Angers (Tours)

Bordeaux

Bordeaux

Caen

Lyon

Jules P. Brateau, Paris, late 19th/20th century

Laurent Morant, Lyon, early 18th century

Bartholomé Leboucq, Lille

242

Bartholomé Leboucq, Lille (town and maker combined in one mark; see also above)

Humbert Leclerc, Lille, 19th century; see also below

Leclerc, Lille, 19th century

LEFEBVRE
A LILLE
Lefebvre, Lille, 19th century

MEUNIER
MARTIN

Martin Meunier, Lille, 19th century

Jacques Nicholas Marchand, Paris, 18th century

Pierre Jouffroy, Besançon, 17th century (incorporating hammer and crown)

Pierre Pissavy, Lyon, 19th century

Germany and Austria–Hungary

Johann Christian Böhme, Freiburg, (master 1755)

Hans Joachim Hansen, Schleswig, 18th century

Johann Gottfried Hütting, Lübeck (master 1802)

Johann Heinrich Isenheim, Strasbourg, 18th century

Johann David Kayser, Stettin, 19th century (town, quality and maker's marks)

Hans Petersen, Lübeck (master 1620)

Nicolaus Kefferlein, Nuremberg, 19th century (one mark incorporates town, quality and maker)

Benjamin Pewes, Danzig (master 1701)

Johann Michael Knoll, Regensburg (master 1796)

Johann Ulrich Koch, Munich (master 1718)

Christoph Ruprecht, Augsburg (master 1718); see also below

Christoph Ruprecht, Augsburg (master 1718); see also above

Benjamin Ferdinand Neumann, Dresden (master 1815)

Philipp Sartori, Vienna, 19th century (town/quality/maker and angel)

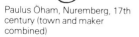

Paulus Öham, Nuremberg, 17th century (town and maker combined)

Johann Wilhelm Schatz, Strasbourg, 18th century

Johann Georg Sibern, Vienna, 18th century

Johann Jacob Sprandel, Ulm, 18th century

Johann Matthias Timmermann, Hamburg, 18th century (quality marks containing maker's initials)

Switzerland

Hans Jakob Basler, Steckborn, late 18th century

quality mark

Lorenzo della Bianca, Wallis (Valais)

PEWTER MARKS

Samuel Bodmer, Berne, 18th century

Hans Heinrich Bosshard, Zurich, 18th century

Franz Joseph Stadler, Uri, early 18th century

Georg Stähelin, St. Gallen, 18th century

Laurenz Wushcer, Schaffhausen, 18th century

Johann Zimmermann, Zurich, 18th century (maker, town and "bodenrosette")

Low Countries

Peter De Buck, Antwerp, 18th century (town mark and quality mark, each with maker's initials)

Arent Jan Coenen, Amsterdam, 18th century (crowned X quality mark and "hallmark")

rose and crown quality mark containing maker's initials I. I.

Piter van Doorn, Utrecht

Jan de Koning, Amsterdam, 18th century (crowned X and "Engels tin" quality; town, and "hallmarks"

Scandinavia

I. G. Ryman, Stockholm, S = date letter for 1776

H. Stichler, Malmö, (master 1752); (maker and town marks combined)

town mark of Norrköping, 18th century

Eric P. Krietz, Stockholm, 18th century

quality mark, 18th century

town marks, 18th century

arms of Sweden, used as a mark of quality

United States of America

Nathaniel Austin, Charlestown, Mass., late 18th/early 19th century

Frederick Bassett, New York and Hartford, 2nd half 18th century

Thomas D. Boardman and Sherman Boardman, Hartford, c. 1810–50

Boardman & Co., New York, c. 1825

Parks Boyd, Philadelphia, late 18th/early 19th century

Joseph Danforth, Middletown, Conn., late 18th century

Thomas Danforth III, Philadelphia, late 18th/early 19th century

Roswell Gleason, Dorchester, Mass., 19th century

Johann Christoph Heyne, Lancaster, Pa., 2nd half 18th century

LEONARD REED & BARTON

Gustavus Leonard, Henry Reed, Charles Barton, Taunton, Mass., 1837–40

William Will Philadelphia, 18th century

Peter Young, New York and Albany, last quarter, 18th century

Art Nouveau and Contemporary

Eduard Hueck, Germany

monogram of the designer Josef Maria Olbrich

"Orion", Germany

Württembergische Metallwarenfabrik (WMF), Germany

HOLLAND
ORANIA
"Orania", Netherlands

245

BIBLIOGRAPHY

Frieder Aichele, *Zinn,* 1977

J. F. F. H. Beeckhuizen, *Tin uit Europese Landen*, 1979

*Belgisch–Nederlands Cultureel Verdrug, *Keur van Tin uit de Havensteden Amsterdam, Antwerpen en Rotterdam* (exhibition catalogue), Amsterdam, 1979

Paul Bidault, *Étains réligieux*, 1978

*Gustav Bossard, *Die Zinngiesser der Schweiz und ihre Werk*, 1920, 1978

Boston Museum of Fine Arts, *American Pewter in the Museum of Fine Arts, Boston*, 1974

Philippe Boucaud and Claude Frégnac, *Les Étains*, 1978

Charles Boucaud, *Les Pichets d'étain, mesures à vin de l'ancienne France*, 1958

Bruckmann, *Zinn Lexikon*, 1977

*Birger Bruzelli, *Tenngjutare i Sverige*, 1967

Shirley Bury, *Victorian Electroplate*, 1971

Shirley Charron, *Modern Pewter, Design and Techniques*, 1974

Michael Clayton, *The Collector's Dictionary of the Silver and Gold of Great Britain and North America*, 1971

*H. H. Cotterell, *Old Pewter: Its Makers and Marks*, 1929, reprinted 1963, 1968

H. H. Cotterell, A. Riff and R. M. Vetter, *National Types of Old Pewter*, 1925, reprinted enlarged 1972

H. H. Cotterell and A. Heal, *Pewterers' Trade Cards*, 1926, 1928

John Culme, *Nineteenth Century Silver*, 1977

B. Douroff, *Étains français des XVIIe et XVIIIe siècles*, 1958

*B. Dubbe, *Tin en Tinnegieters in Nederland*, 1965

J. Fleming and H. Honour, *The Penguin Dictionary of Decorative Arts*, 1977

Johannes Gahlnbäck, *Russisches Zinn*, 1928

Philippe Garner (ed.), *Phaidon Encyclopedia of the Decorative Arts, 1890–1940*, 1978

Hans-Ulrich Haedeke, *Metalwork*, 1970

Hans-Ulrich Haedeke, *Zinn*, 1973

J. Hatcher and T. C. Barker, *A History of British Pewter*, 1974

*Erwin Hintze, *Die Deutschen Zinngiesser und Ihre Marken*, 7 vols., 1921–6, reprinted 1964

R. F. Homer, *Five Centuries of Base Metal Spoons*, 1975

International Tin Research Institute, London, *Working with Pewter*, 1979

Radway Jackson, *English Pewter Touchmarks*, edited and with an introduction by R. G. Michaelis, 1970

Carl Jacobs, *A Guide to American Pewter*, 1957

J. B. Kerfoot, *American Pewter*, 1924, reprinted 1942

*Theodore Kohlmann, *Zinngiesse Handwerk und Zinngerät in Oldenburg, Ostfriesland und Osnabrück*, 1972

*Ledlie Irwin Laughlin, *Pewter in America: Its Makers and their Marks*, 2 vols., 1940, reprinted 1 vol. 1969, updating volume 1970

H. J. L. Massé (1921) revised R. F. Michaelis, *The Pewter Collector*, 1971

R. F. Michaelis, *Antique Pewter of the British Isles*, 1955, 1971

R. F. Michaelis, *British Pewter*, 1969

R. F. Michaelis, *Old Domestic Base Metal Candlesticks*, 1978

*Charles F. Montgomery, *A History of American Pewter*, 1973, new edn 1978

Ludwig Mory, *Schönes Zinn*, 1964

Christopher A. Peal, *British Pewter and Britannia Metal*, 1971

*Christopher A. Peal, *More Pewter Marks* (and addenda), 1976, 1977

Margaret Pieper-Lippe, *Zinn im Südlichen Westfalen*, 1974

Adolphe Riff, *Les Étains strasbourgeois du XVIe au XIXe siècle*, 1925

B. O. Santesson, *Gammalt Tenn*, 1963

*Hugo Schneider, *Zinn, Katalog der Sammlung des Schweizerischen Landesmuseums, Zurich*, 1970

*Tardy, *Les Étains français*, 1964

*Tardy, *Les Poinçons des étains français*, 1967

A. J. Tilbrook, *The Designs of Archibald Knox for Liberty & Co.*, 1976

*Friederich Tischer, *Bohmisches Zinn und Seine Marken*, 1973

A. J. G. Verster, *Tin door de Eeuwen*, 1954 (trs. as *Old European Pewter*, 1958)

R. M. Vetter and G. Wacha, *Linzer Zinngiesser*, 1967

Piroska Weiner, *Old Pewter in Hungarian Collections*, tr. from Hungarian, 1971

S. C. Woolmer and C. H. Arkwright, *Pewter of the Channel Islands*, 1973

Worshipful Company of Pewterers, *Catalogue of Pewter in its Possession*, 1968 and 1979

Yale University, *American Pewter, Garvan and Other Collections at Yale*, 1965

Rolando van Zeller, *Estanhos Portugueses*, 1969

*Books recommended for tracing marks, although many others listed include a selection.

GLOSSARY

Note: Terms relating to pewter marks are discussed in the chapter on Marks. The descriptive terms for different forms of thumbpiece, handle, spoon finial etc. are discussed in the Introduction.

Annealing. Method of toughening objects (especially in the making of silver) whereby metal is heated and slowly cooled while hammered into shape

Arabesque. Entwined decoration, incorporating principally foliage and strapwork

Auricular. Style of goldsmiths in Low Countries in the 17th century, incorporating curved forms resembling the inside of the human ear (hence the name)

Baluster. A shape (e.g. of old measures) in which the curved outline broadens above the foot and narrows towards the neck

Baroque. Style most influential in the 17th century; its chief characteristic is bold, flamboyant decoration using scrolling foliage, shells and figures in extravagant fashion

Bénitier. (French) holy-water stoup

Biedermeier. Style (chiefly in furniture) fashionable c. 1820–50 in Austria and Germany

Bifurcated. Divided into two — usually refers to thumbpieces

Black metal. Pewter of low grade with up to 30–40% lead

Bleeding bowl. Sometimes confused with porringer; the medical instrument had markings inside the bowl

Bombé shape. Term derived from furniture (especially a chest of drawers) to describe a swelling convex curved outline

Booge. Curved section of a plate or bowl below the border

Boss. Domed circular part in centre of plate or dish

Brandy bowl. Term used for the Dutch equivalent of an écuelle or two-handled porringer

Brass. Alloy of (chiefly) copper and zinc

Britannia metal. A "hard metal" alloy of tin (approx. 90%) and antimony, most popular in the 19th century

Broken. A design of handle also known as double-scroll

Bronze. Alloy of copper and tin

Burette. (French) altar cruet, to contain wine and/or water

Capstan shape. A cylindrical or oblong convex form based on the ship's capstan (e.g. of early 18th-century salts)

Caryatid. Female figure used as a support, as in architecture, or a handle

Casting. The traditional method of forming an object by pouring molten metal into a mould

Caudle cup. Two-handled bowl or cup, often with cover, in which was served posset or caudle; also known as a porringer. *See* Écuelle

Chasing. Decoration in relief achieved by using a hammer and punch; the term covers both embossing and repoussé

Chrismatory. Vessel which contains holy oil

Crest. Heraldic device placed above a coat of arms, often engraved on its own to signify ownership

Cruet. Vessel to contain communion wine or water (altar cruet); a group of bottles and casters containing salt, pepper, ginger, mustard and sauces, often including a cruet frame

Dinanderie. Brassware from Dinant, near Liège

Display pewter. Highly decorated pewter made for show rather than use

Drip-pan. Disc projecting from the stem of a candlestick to catch molten wax

Ear. Flat handle, as on porringers or écuelles

Écuelle. (French) shallow bowl with two handles and usually a cover. *See* Porringer

Edelzinn. Display pewter cast in relief; used since the 19th century to describe German and French relief pewter of 16th and 17th centuries

Embossing. Raised decoration achieved by hammering from the back. *See* Chasing, Repoussé

Empire style. Development of neo-classicism of the Napoleonic era, about 1800–25

Enamel. Colourful semi-transparent vitreous substance used to decorate metal; seldom used on pewter; methods include champlevé, cloisonné, plique à jour

Englisch Zinn. Metal purified to English standards, or using English tin. *See* Feinzinn

Engraving. Method of decoration by which metal is incised in lines with a tool called a burin. *See* Wrigglework

Excise mark. Stamp to show that duty has been paid on an item

Feinzinn. Pewter of high quality

Finial. Topmost feature of a piece, particularly a spoon, or centring the lid of a measure or flagon

Flagon. Vessel for pouring liquid, but not of a fixed or official capacity. A flagon is generally larger than a measure, usually lidded and with a handle, and with or without a spout

Flatware. An overall term for pewter plates, dishes and chargers; (also applied to silver knives, forks and spoons)

Fluting. Shallow incurved grooves, used vertically or spirally, as a decorative feature. *See* Lobing

Gadroon. Border decoration of convex curved forms or inverted fluting etc.

Garnish. Set of pewter tableware, including dishes, plates, and sometimes soup tureens, sauceboats, ladles etc.

Girdle. Moulded band encircling the body of an object

Grotesques. Fanciful and intricate designs loosely incorporating human figures, sphinxes, animals, foliage etc., derived in the 16th century from Roman originals

Guild. Society whose members belong to the same trade; in England known as a livery company

Gun metal. *See* Bronze

GLOSSARY

Hammering. A method of working pewter intended to strengthen it; the imparting of a "hammered" finish by beating with a small hammer

Hard metal. Tin alloy containing only a small proportion of lead, if any. *See* Britannia metal

Hollow-ware. Vessels made to contain liquid, e.g. measures, flagons, tankards, mugs

Housemark. Non-heraldic device stamped or engraved to signify ownership

Imperial Standard. Scale of capacity measures introduced in the British Isles in 1826

Incuse. Stamped into the metal

Japanning. See Lacquer

Knop. Finial; also an abrupt widening in the middle of the stem of a chalice, cup or candlestick

Lacquer. Colourful varnish used to decorate furniture and metalwork, a practice of oriental origin

Latten. Brass

Laver. Vessel used to contain water for washing

Lay metal. Pewter not of the finest quality, usually used for hollow-ware

Livery Company. See Guild

Lobing. Broad convex curves used to decorate a surface

Mannerism. A style which followed that of the Renaissance, in the 16th and early 17th centuries; characterized by sinuous human and animal forms linked by foliage, strapwork and grotesques (e.g. Briot)

Measure. A vessel of traditional local form and capacity usually with lid, thumbpiece and handle, used for measuring or serving liquid

Mug. Lidless drinking vessel with a side handle

Mutchkin. Scots measure equivalent to ¾ Imperial pint

Neo-classical. Style originating in France and England in the 1750s, then spreading to the rest of Europe and North America; a reaction to rococo, using classical ornament

Noggin. Measure equal to a gill (¼ pint)

O.E.W.S. Old English Wine Standard; pre-Imperial capacity

Pichet. (French) general term for measure

Pilgrim bottle. Flattened pear-shaped vessel carried by means of a strap or chain — developed into an item for display rather than use

Pitcher. In the U.S.A. a broad-lipped jug for cream or, larger and lidded or unlidded, for cider or water

Plouk. Small lump of metal inside a measure which indicates capacity

Porringer. Circular shallow bowl with a single ear, sometimes called a bleeding bowl

Pot. Capacity equivalent to two quarts

Pricket. Candlestick with spike onto which the candle is stuck

Punch. Tool used to stamp a mark or design into metal; hence punched or stamped ornament

Pyx. Container for the consecrated sacrament of communion

Reeding. Decoration by incised or cast moulded bands, chiefly at the rim of plates and dishes; hence single-reeded, triple-reeded, multiple-reeded

Repoussé. Relief work executed by hammering from the front of a piece. *See* Embossing

Rocaille. Ornament using forms derived from shells and rockwork, especially popular in rococo style

Rococo. Style fashionable about 1720–70; assymetrical, chiefly incorporating scrolls, shells, foliage and rocaille ornament

Sadware. Overall term for plates, dishes and chargers

Sconce. Upper part of a candlestick into which the candle fits; wall sconces incorporate a plate which acts as reflector

Scrolls, scrolling. Forms of decoration and in handles, etc., characteristic of rococo and some domestic ware

Serpentine. Stone containing chrysotile and antigorite, usually dark green

Skirt base. Chiefly on flagons and tankards, flaring outwards to raise the body from table level

Spinning. Process by which sheet metal is turned on a lathe, usually over a wooden "chuck", to form it into the desired shape

Stamped ornament. See Punch

Stitze. (German) general term for a flagon, but usually one of slender cylindrical form, slightly flared at the base

Straight-fold. Vertical moulding, characteristic of early German (1720–40) and of Low Countries rococo ware

Strapwork. Ornament of interwoven bands. *See* Arabesque

Tankard. Drinking vessel with a lid and handle

Tappit-hen. Scottish measure of a particular design

Tin pest. Corrosion of tin due to cold or to atmospheric conditions; the metal becomes bubbly on the surface and gradually disintegrates

Touchplate. The touchplate is the sheet of metal on which a pewterer registers his mark (touch) on becoming a master

Trefid spoon. Late 17th- and early 18th-century design, the flattened terminal divided into three parts

Trencher salt. Small salt, concave at top to hold the salt; placed beside individual plates; 17th and early 18th century

Tulip-shape. Baluster-shaped; usually applied to mugs and tankards

Volute. Spiral scroll

Wrigglework. Zig-zag engraving, achieved by moving the burin in a rocking movement; popular in the late 17th and first half of the 18th century

Wrythen. Flame-like (e.g. of spoon finials)

ACKNOWLEDGEMENTS

Photographs were supplied by the American Museum in Britain, Bath on pp. 175, 176, 177b, 178, 181, 182, 184b, 187t, 187b, 188, 236br; Amsterdam Historical Museum 146; Shirley Charron 224b; The Connoisseur 224t; Alain Henry 226; © International Tin Research Institute 15t, 228; © International Tin Research Institute, courtesy Abbey Pewter Ltd, London 14t, 14b, 15b; Musée de l'Hospice Comtesse, Lille, 230; Mansell Collection 16; Hein Molenaar 227t; Zinngiesserei Ludwig Mory, Munich 229; The New-York Historical Society 173; Arne Brunn Rasmussen, Copenhagen 162, 166, 167t, 167b; Rijksmuseum, Amsterdam 142; Ann Ronan Picture Library 10, 92; Sotheby's Belgravia 211, 212, 213, 216, 217t, 217b, 218, 220, 221; Sotheby Parke Bernet & Co., London 9, 28l, 28r, 29l, 38, 46b, 50, 51, 58t, 59, 63t, 64, 82, 98, 99, 100, 103, 118–119, 122, 125, 127r, 129, 136, 152, 160, 165b; Sotheby Parke Bernet, New York 184t, 186; Svenskt Tenn, Stockholm 227b; Henry Francis du Pont Winterthur Museum Inc. 177t, 180, 185, 189.

Pewter was made available for photography by St. Bartholomew's Hospital, London 19b; Robin Bellamy, Witney 36tl, 36cl, 36cr, 36br, 52b, 58b, 61t, 63br, 108b, 109, 111; Bethnal Green Museum, London 90, 214, 215t, 215b, 219; Boorer collection 46t, 60, 200t; Jack Casimir Ltd, London 52t, 83, 134, 143tr, 164, 183, 195, 196t, 197, 198, 199t, 200b, 201, 202b, 203, 204b, 205b, 208, 236bl; Christie, Manson & Woods, London 31t, 127l, 149; Dirven collection 18, 21, 22t, 22b, 26, 30b, 31br, 42, 43, 70, 72, 75t, 77, 79, 97t, 97b, 105t, 108t, 112, 131, 132, 138, 147, 148, 150, 155, 159t, 159b, 168, 232bl, 232br; Hempson of Mount St, London 94, 107l, 115, 128, 157; Phillips, London 30t, 33, 37, 75b, 106, 114bl, 158, 192l, 192r, 196b, 209, 233tr, 236tr, 237b; Royal Copenhagen Porcelain and Georg Jenson Silver Ltd 222, 223t, 223b, 225, 237tl, 237tr; Sotheby Parke Bernet & Co., London 2, 8, 11, 19t, 32, 34, 36tr, 36bl, 48br, 101, 56, 61b, 62, 63bl, 67t, 73, 74, 76, 80, 81, 93, 95, 102, 104, 105b, 110, 113, 114br, 124, 130, 135, 137tl, 153, 156, 193, 194, 199b, 202t, 205t, 206, 207, 233t, 233b, 236tl; Victoria and Albert Museum, London 17, 23, 41t, 84, 116, 165t; David Walter-Ellis 31bl, 86; The Worshipful Company of Pewterers, London 6, 40; other private collections 29t, 29br, 41b, 48t, 48bl, 49, 57, 66, 67b, 78, 87, 107r, 114t, 120, 133, 137b, 139, 151, 154, 169, 204t, 232tl, 232tr.

ACKNOWLEDGEMENTS

Special photography by A. C. Cooper, London and Paul Forrester, London: A. C. Cooper 2, 6, 8, 11, 17, 19*t*, 23, 29*t*, 30*t*, 32, 33, 34, 36*tr*, 36*bl*, 37, 40, 41*t*, 48*b*, 53, 56, 61*b*, 62, 63*bl*, 67*t*, 73, 74, 75*b*, 76, 80, 81, 84, 86, 90, 93, 94, 95, 101, 102, 104, 105*b*, 106, 107, 110, 113, 114*b*, 115, 116, 124, 127*l*, 128, 130, 135, 137*t*, 153, 154, 156, 157, 158, 165*t*, 192*l*, 193, 194, 199*b*, 202*t*, 205*t*, 206, 207, 209, 214, 215*t*, 215*b*, 219, 222, 223*t*, 223*b*, 225, 232*tl*, 232*tr*, 233*b*, 233*tr*, 236*tl*, 237*tl*, 237tr, 237*b*; Paul Forrester 18, 19*b*, 21, 22*t*, 22*b*, 26, 29*br*, 30*b*, 31*t*, 31*bl*, 31*br*, 36*tl*, 36*cl*, 36*cr*, 36*br*, 41*b*, 42, 43, 46*t*, 48*t*, 49, 52*t*, 52*b*, 57, 58*b*, 60, 61*t*, 63*br*, 66, 67*b*, 70, 72, 75*t*, 77, 78, 79, 83, 87, 97*t*, 97*b*, 105*t*, 108*t*, 108*b*, 109, 111, 112, 114*t*, 120, 131, 132, 133, 134, 137*b*, 138, 139, 143*tr*, 147, 148, 149, 150, 151, 155, 159*t*, 159*b*, 164, 168, 169, 183, 192*r*, 195, 196, 197, 198, 199*t*, 200*t*, 200*b*, 201, 202*b*, 203, 204*t*, 204*b*, 205*b*, 208, 232*bl*, 232*br*, 233*tr*, 236*tr*, 236*bl*.

All the drawings of pewter are by John Fuller, the marks by John Brennan and the maps by Liz Orrock and Zoë Goodwin.

INDEX

Numbers in *italic* indicate illustrations

INDEX